Preyed Upon by A Predator
Bruised, Broken, & Saved

By

Julee Kay

Prologue

My name is Julee Kay. Everything in this book is true. These events happened to me. I did not exaggerate anything because I didn't have to. I recounted them just the way they happened. I'm sharing these things in hopes that it will help another person who is living a life in hell. I hope that it shows them that they are strong enough to change their situation. I know how hard it is. The fear of telling others about what is going on stops us from speaking up along with that overwhelming feeling of shame that we carry. We feel ashamed and don't want others to know what we have endured. I just want to tell you that you have nothing to be ashamed of, it's not your fault. I know you say to yourself that they will look at you and ask, why you stayed. That is a hard question to answer, and everyone's answer is different. Don't let their judgment keep you from seeking help.

THE FIRST DATE

It was December 2012, and my life was in shambles. I had married Joe. A man much older than me and none of his family approved. They did everything they could to tear us apart. We didn't let anybody know about it for a long time, and he decided he was going to do what he wanted no matter what they said or did.

So, we let everyone know and got married on January 20th, 2012. His family wouldn't leave us alone; they always put doubt in his mind. He loved me for me. Not for what I had or what I could do but me. He was my best friend. He meant more to me than anyone could ever know. He made me feel alive because for once in my life I felt like someone really, and actually loved me.

His family finally won out, and he filed for divorce the day before Thanksgiving. I didn't know until the Monday after Thanksgiving. I was devastated. I turned to the internet to escape and signed up on a dating site called Plentyoffish.com or POF.

I sat in the guest bedroom day after day in disbelief of what was going on. I was also furious because once again I was being thrown away. It made me feel that I was unlovable and worthless. Once again, I had failed, and I have to start my life all over again. It's not the first time, I have had to start over more times than I want to count.

I began reading profiles on the dating site. A few people messaged me, and I began to have conversations with them. They helped to remove some of my sadness and despair. I went on a couple of dates, and all I could think about was Joe sitting at home alone. I talked to Blane for a couple of weeks before we went on our first date. I was really excited about this date because he was funny and made me laugh and it took my mind off of what was happening at home.

It was January 13, 2013; I was getting ready to meet Blane for lunch at Little America. My stomach hurt so bad, I thought about canceling the date, but I have a thing about keeping my commitments because if I say I'm going to be there or do something, I do it. I have been flaked on too many times in my life and know what it feels like to be let down, and I don't want to be that kind of person.

I arrived at the restaurant. Blane was already waiting for me. He greeted me with a large smile, and I could see he was missing a couple of teeth on his lower right side. He was 5' 6", about 160 pounds, short brown hair, thick mustache and brown eyes. I thought Wow he has beautiful eyes they sparkled, reminding me of someone else's eyes but at the time I couldn't remember whose, I did eventually remember, and I think that was something that drew me to him.

We were escorted to the table, and he pulled out my chair for me and then sat across from me. My stomach was still bothering me. I tried to not think about it, but it just seemed to get more painful. I don't know if it was because I ate something that didn't agree with me or if it was all the stress from the divorce I was going through? I ordered a BLT even though I didn't want anything to eat, and he ordered a club sandwich. I ordered water. He told me, "Go ahead and order a soda if you want." I said that I was giving up soft drinks. Funny how many times I have quit drinking soda and then picked it back up again.

It's like that with a lot of things. I have smoked and quit half-dozen time. At this time, I was a non-smoker, but unfortunately, I started to smoke again when everything began falling apart. He started telling me that he picked this restaurant because his grandfather helped build it.

He was so proud of that and talked on and on about how his Dad and grandfather had built a lucrative construction business and how he was going to take over the business. He said he was working with his Dad, but things had been so slow that he was doing some temp jobs to keep him busy until things picked up.

We discovered that we both attended the same church, and we talked about what a great pastor we had and how much we enjoyed his sermons. He told me about his kids and glowed as he talked about how successful they were.

He seemed like such a nice guy. His eyes were very kind, and he listened attentively to me, as I told him about my children and grandchildren.

I told him about my oldest daughter and how she was a massage therapist, and he said he could use a massage because his back had been bothering him. I gave him her number so he could book an appointment. I was always letting people know about her because she was excellent and was trying to build her business.

I barely ate my sandwich and asked for a box to take it. He ate all of his, and I probably would have done the same if my stomach weren't so upset. He walked me to my car, and we stood there for a few minutes and talked. We said goodbye, and he said he was going to call and schedule an appointment with my daughter.

On the drive home, I thought about our date and wondered if I would hear from him. I enjoyed myself and thought he seemed like a nice guy. I didn't think he was that good looking, but I also didn't think he was ugly. He was average but did have a pleasant personality.

I got home and when I walked in, Joe was sitting in his usual spot in his large brown Lazy Boy recliner with his dog Russy, a black poodle who weighed about 20 pounds, lying next to him, between his leg and the arm of the chair. He was always either next to Joe or following close behind him. You could tell that they loved each other, and one would be lost, without the other.

He smiled at me, but I could see the sadness in his eyes. I know he still loved me and I still loved him. I have never stopped loving Joe. I went into my room and cried because it hurt so much to see the pain in his eyes. Neither one of us wanted to go our separate ways, but his family just wouldn't leave us alone. There were also some other things that were driving a wedge between us.

TO THE RESCUE

Early the next morning my phone rang and it was Blane. He said his van wouldn't start and it was his first day at the Outdoors Expo downtown. He sounded desperate, so I offered him a ride. I took my kids to school and then I went and gave him a ride to his job. He asked if I could pick him up after and I said that I would. I picked him up, and I asked him if he wanted me to take him to get the part for his van. He said he didn't have the money to get it until he got paid and I offered to buy it for him. He said that it would be awesome and he would pay me back when he got paid.

I took him to Napa Auto Parts, and we purchased a fuel filter for his van. He knew that was what the problem was because he had had the same problem for a while.

He put his arm around my shoulder as we stood in line waiting for the part. It felt nice. I gave him a ride back home. He lived in an apartment over a large shop. His Dad owned the building.

When you enter the building, you will go into a large room that had display cases with model cars and some other knick-knacks. There was a desk on the left behind one of the display cases. On the right was his Dad's office. If you walked straight ahead, there was an office, and one on the left and two more down the hall. A large chandelier hung in the middle of the room, and three windows above the light went into Blane's apartment. Once you walked in the main door, you would immediately turn to your left and go through the door. As soon as you stepped through the door, there was a flight of stairs leading to his apartment.

In the area where the stairs were, there were three bays to work on cars. Blane's Dad had an antique car in the first spot. The other had Blane's van, and the last one had a ton of junk. A bathroom which had a toilet and a sink was greasy, and dirty and smelled like urine. It was evident that no one had cleaned it in some time. Thirteen stairs up to his loft. Once you got to the top and stepped inside, the bathroom is right in front of you. The sink and mirror were the first things you see, to the left there's the shower and the toilet right next to it, and a stackable washer and dryer. He kept his laundry supplies, on a ledge.

When you come through the door and turn to your right you enter the kitchen, and to your left is a long counter with the stove and sink. The refrigerator is directly in front of you when you turn to your left while walking in the door. There were a large oval table and six chairs.

After passing the table, you come to the living room. The tan suede couch has big cushions that swallow you up, making it is so hard to get up. There's a square coffee table in front of the sofa, and there were always receipts, spare change and a tool or two on it. Also in the living room, there are windows on each side of the TV.

Directly in front of the coffee table, about four feet way is a stereo system with a large flat screen TV. To the left is a green plaid love seat, and directly across are two recliner chairs. Behind them some room dividers. On the other side of the dividers were two dressers and two steps from there was a large four poster bed with a large headboard, an end table on each side with large windows above them, and a larger dresser with a mirror on the left side against the wall between two windows. Directly in front of the bed is a weight bench with weights and another weight lifting stuff. All along the wall going down to from the kitchen to the living room was a shelf that stuck out four feet and windows.

I took the tour of his place and then told him I had to go.

I have described his apartment in detail because this is where most of the nightmare took place. A place I never want to step foot in again.

I needed to get home to my kids. I didn't like leaving them alone at Joe's with everything that was going on with the divorce. Things had been very tense between him and my children. They never saw eye to eye. He was from a different era and didn't understand or like a lot of what my kids did. At times, they were very disrespectful to me, and that made him angry. So, I hurried home, and my kids were downstairs watching TV. I was so relieved that there had been no problems in my absence.

DROPPED A BOMB

I met Blane at his apartment. We were going out to dinner and a movie. This evening was only our second real date. I didn't count taking him to work and picking him up a date. We hadn't decided what we were going to see. We figured we would just pick something when we got there, which was OK with me. I'm not too picky when it comes to movies, I enjoy all different kinds, which makes taking me to the movies easy.

We took his van. The inside of the van was a mess, and all the wires were hanging all over the place. He said his brother Dale had done that when he had the van, Blane hadn't had the time to fix it.

As we were driving along the I-15 going to Jordan Landing, he suddenly said to me. "I am a registered sex offender. My ex said that I victimized her children. I didn't do it. She was angry and trying to get even with me. I was innocent, but they still convicted me."

I froze and didn't say anything.

He said, "You're awfully quiet."

I said, "Yea sorry." That just shocked me and took me by surprise. I know how some women can do that out of vengeance, and it really must suck.

He said, "Yes, it did, and it wasn't fair that he had to go to prison for a crime he didn't commit."

We proceeded to go to a sports bar, where we had dinner. It was so much fun we laughed and joked. I had a Long Beach, and he had a Crown and Coke. It only takes one drink for me to get tipsy.

As we walked over to the theater, I tripped and almost fell. Blane caught me. I laughed to cover my embarrassment. We watched the movie. I can't remember what we saw. It must not have been that good.

The ride back to his house seemed like it was taking forever. Neither one of us said much. When we got to his house, he asked if I wanted to come up for a minute. I said sure and went upstairs. We sat next to each other on the brown couch.

He leaned over and kissed me, his hand on my shoulder. He ran his hand down my arm.

I pulled back and said I had to go. Blane didn't try to convince me to stay or push himself on me. He said, "I don't want you to do anything that you don't want to do." He seemed like such a gentleman. He walked me down to my car, gave me a hug and said he had a great time.

I told him, "Thank you. I had a wonderful time too."

On my drive home, I thought about what he had told me. I know how a woman can do those things when they have been betrayed and hurt, and I also know that innocent people go to jail. I know this first hand, so I believed him.

I also thought, he just met me and he told me this, so it gave me a false sense of trust. I mean if someone if going to come right out with something like that they must be trustworthy.

He called me the next day and said he was going to St. George for the weekend to help his Dad work on his house, and that he would pay me back for the part when he returned. His Dad owned a home there as well, and they spent time in both places. I told him to have a good time and be safe.

Joe

On January 10th, 2013 Joe and I met at my attorney's office to do mediation. We agreed on a settlement that said I would move out of the house by January 31. For several weeks, I packed boxes and took them to my house. I spent most of the weekend, when Blane was in St George, packing and taking what I could to my house.

Joe had answered an ad I had in the Salt Lake Tribune for house cleaning in 2008. I cleaned for him for a short time. He would call me whenever he needed his house done. Then I didn't hear from him for a long time.

I happened to be working in his area one day and decided to stop by and see how he was doing and if he needed my services. He said he was glad to see me and did need my help.
I scheduled a cleaning, then my partner Kelly and I cleaned his house. He rebooked for two weeks later.

After I had gone back a few times, he called me and asked if I would be willing to go out to dinner with him. I said I saw no harm in it. I know that he was very lonely because his wife had died not too long before I had originally started working for him. He had often told me when I was working for him, that his children didn't come around very much. We went to dinner, and he talked a lot about his wife who had passed. He asked how my business was going and I told him about a few of my clients that made me crazy. He laughed and asked if he was one of them.

He would ask me out to dinner or breakfast every couple of weeks, and I would gladly accept. One time when I was cleaning his house, he told me to look in his room. I did, but I didn't know what I was supposed to be looking for, so I went back out to the living room and asked what was I looking for.

He laughed and got up, and we headed to his room. Standing up next to the mirrored closet door was a fishing pole. He grabbed the pole and said that his kid had given it to him. I said that was cool and asked when he was going to go fishing. His smile faded, and he said he didn't have anyone to go with him. I said, "I will go fishing with you." He got the biggest smile on his face and said, "Really you'll go fishing with me." "Yes, Joe, I will. Just plan it and let me know."

The next Saturday we went to Jordanelle Reservoir. He seemed happier than I had ever seen him. He showed me how to put the hook on the line, put on my weights, what bait to use. We got our lawn chairs out and tied Russy to one of the chairs because he wanted to explore, but we didn't want him to get lost or bother any of the fishermen. We spent several hours just fishing and relaxing. We didn't catch anything but still thoroughly enjoyed ourselves.

On the drive home, I got cold, and I placed the afghan that was laying on the back seat on my lap. Russy jumped over the seat and curled up on my lap. Then he decided he wanted to look out of the window. Suddenly my lap became very warm, and I realized that he had peed on me.

"Oh!! my God Joe Russy just peed on me." I screamed.

I grabbed a towel and started cleaning it up. We were both laughing hysterically. I nicknamed Russy, Mr. Peebody. Joe asked if we could go fishing again and I said that would be great. I would like to bring my son with me next time, and he thought that would work.

The next time we went fishing, I took my son Bennett. Bennett didn't want to fish. He wanted to walk down the trail and go exploring. So, we did just Bennett and me. We played along the edge, where there was a five-foot drop to the water. I kept telling Ben to be careful not to get too close. I'm such a worry-wart.

We tried skipping rocks but never did get any to skip. We went back, and Joe was relaxing in his lawn chair, fishing. Once again, we didn't catch anything but just being out there enjoying the beauty and the fresh air was well worth the drive up. Joe and Bennett got along great. Joe told me he really enjoyed spending the day with us and that he really liked Ben.

Joe asked me to come over many times and have dinner and visit. On one of my visits, he surprised me with a bulb and a lens cover for my blazer. I had been hit in the back and hadn't fixed it. He said it was unsafe to have the brake light out and we need to fix it. He had been a mechanic for a large part of his life. He had me do it as he explained it to me. I really didn't need him to, but I let him tell me anyway.

He couldn't do it because of arthritis in his hands, and he had a hard time with the little screws. I had a hard time holding on to the screws too.

I really enjoyed being over there. We would talk about his life and all the things he had done, about his wife and his children. Joe was so lonely, and well, I was too. I had been single since 2006 and didn't have much of a social life, so it was awesome to have someone to hang out with even though he was much older than me.

Age didn't matter to us. We just enjoyed each other's company, but we both knew that no one else would understand, that was why we kept our friendship a secret. Joe was about five feet, six inches and weighed about 160 lbs. His hair, what he had left of it, was gray and he had a gray beard. He was handsome for a man his age. But I was not physically attracted to him. I just loved his company and all the stories he would tell me.

I remember one day he asked me if I wanted a milk nickel. A what?

"A milk nickel."

I said, "Hmm, sure."

He told me to go to the freezer that it was in there. I looked at him like he was nuts and he started laughing. I looked but didn't know what I was looking for.

He said, "Grab one of those ice creams." I did.

He said, "That is a milk nickel. Back in my day they cost a nickel and were made from milk, and that is where it got its name". I laughed at myself because I should have figured it out but didn't.

That's just an example of one of our conversations. We had so many enjoyable conversations; I learned a lot about the history of our country from his stories.

On December 24th of 2011, I stayed overnight at his house for the very first time. My oldest son stayed with me because we were going skiing up at Brighton Ski Resort the next morning. The three of us shared a lovely dinner and turned in early so we could get up early. The next morning Joe's grandson and his wife and their little girl showed up. Joe and I were making breakfast, and his granddaughter commented that we seemed like an old married couple with the way we were behaving. We just looked at each other and smiled.

Nobody knew about the time we had been spending, so it was kind of funny to us. I had only met his grandson and granddaughter once. They showed up to mow his lawn when my employee and I was there cleaning.

We started spending more time together, and he called me daily. It was crazy, but I looked forward to seeing him. He was my best friend, and I loved him.

One day after we had gone to dinner we were driving to his house, and he looked over at me when I was stopped at the light and said, "Marry me."

I said, "What did you say"?

He said, "Marry me."

I replied that I would have to ask my children. They are part of me, and it would affect their lives as well. "What about your kids? You know they will freak out, they don't even know about us, and all the time we have spent together".

He said, "Don't worry about them"?

I told my kids that Joe asked me to marry him and they were like, "Mom, he is as old as dirt. Why would you want to marry him"?

Here is where I need to be honest because I am no saint. Joe lived in an enormous, beautiful house in Cottonwood Heights. The schools were some of the best in the state. So, yeah, my kids would be going to better schools. I wouldn't have to work as hard. I would have an easier life. So, that played into my decision, but I also enjoyed being with Joe, so that made it even easier.

Everybody thought I was only in it for what I could get. They didn't know or understand what we had. We got married January 20th, 2012. I didn't move in until June because I didn't want to take my kids out of school in the middle of the year and they didn't want to have to change schools either.

I spent weekends at Joe's. We cooked together, went out to eat, and took advantage of the time we had.

One evening in February he called me and asked if I could come over he said it was important and he had to talk to me. It couldn't wait.

I didn't see him very often during the week because I had to take my daughter, Harmony to gymnastics, and do other household duties, and I would be tired. It seemed like it was urgent for him, so I hurried over to see what the deal was.

He told me to go in the guest room and look at the computer. It had a picture of a gray minivan. He came up behind me.

He said, "I want to buy that for you."

I said, "Joe, you don't need to do that."

He said, "I know. I want to. Come on let's go see about getting you that van".

I was so excited. I asked him why he had decided to buy this for me.

He said, "I would feel better knowing you are driving around in a dependable vehicle. You drive a lot, and I want you to be safe".

I saw a side of him at the dealership that I had never seen before. He told them what he was willing to pay and not a penny more. They tried to get him to change his mind, but he stood firm. We got up to leave. I was really bummed out. I fell in love with the van and really wanted it, but you don't always get what you want. Hey, isn't that a title of a very famous song?

As we were walking to the car, the salesman came running after us. As usual, they gave us the song and dance; Oh, after talking to the big guy, blah blah. They had decided to let us have it for that price.

I was jumping for joy on the inside. I had never been given such an amazing gift.

The next month he totally surprised me again. I was sitting on the couch at his house, and he walked over, got on his knees in front of me, took my hand into his hands, and said, "Julee I love you so much. You are my world, and I wish I could give you the world. I don't have a lot, but what I do have I want you to have. I'm giving you the house; I want you to have it when I die".

I said, "I don't think your kids are going to like that.

He said, "Don't worry about them they don't want it, and I will handle it if there are any problems."

WOW! He wanted me to have this amazing house.

It had a three-car garage. I usually entered through the garage. When you get out of the car, there is a ramp that leads to the house. When you enter, you go into the laundry room which had been remodeled to add an open shower, toilet, and sink. It had been renovated for his deceased wife because she had a stroke and they needed to be able to take care of her. Once you exit the laundry room, you step into the dining room, from there you could see the kitchen, living room and stairs.

As you walk through the living room to the hall, there is a large beautiful bathroom on your left. Directly across the hall is a guest room with a computer. Next to that room is another room, and across from there, a very large bedroom with mirror closet doors and a small bathroom. That was Joe's room.

His room had a king size bed, an end table on each side, windows all along the south side wall. At the foot of the bed, he had a long bench seat and a dresser right in front of it.

The front door points to the north, and the staircase is direct across from the front door. At the bottom of the stairs, you enter into a very vast area that has white tile. To your left is a bathroom, and next to that; a room he had been using to do his silversmith stuff. Across from the bathroom is a large room with a pool table and windows all along the north wall. When you turn right from the bottom of the stairs, you come to a very large living room. It was a beautiful house but did need some changes. Like the drapes. They were floral and just needed to go they screamed old.

I sat in shock when he told me this. I knew he loved me and was always doing things to show me that. No one had every cared about me as much as he did. I had finally found someone who really and truly loved me.

When we moved in it was OK at first, but things started getting difficult. Joe, would want to take me to dinner and not take the kids because he wanted me all to himself.

My kids began to resent him. He would become irritated if I would go downstairs and hang out with my kids. He would get mad if I went somewhere with the kids.

I had never seen this side of Joe. He became very possessive. The kids started resenting him and felt like he had taken their mother away from them.

He wanted me to just sit there in that recliner and rot. I tried to involve him with my family. On Mother's Day, my daughter was having a BBQ for me, and I invited him. He came but sulked the whole time. We all hung out at the pool. Joe was mad because I had him bring his car because I knew he would want to go home and call it a day before me, so that was why he was sulking.

I planned a day at that lake in July, and he didn't want to come because he said it would be hot and he didn't want to be out there all day. I went ahead anyway.

I got a phone call while I was there. He was at home with his kids. I could hear them in the background, and one of them said, "She should be here at home. She is your wife, and this is where she should be and not at the lake".

I immediately got angry. I had a family, and I was not going just to sit there and not be part of their lives. His kids thought I should just be a wife and close the door on my children. I guess that is how people of that generation think, and well; it is wrong.

The kids started school in August. Bennett loved his new school and made friends quickly, which is kind of amazing because he never was really good at making friends. Harmony, on the other hand, hated her school and sat under a tree the whole year by herself. She didn't make any new friends. She became very depressed and used food as a coping skill. She put on a lot of weight. She had been in great shape when we moved over there because she did gymnastics two to three times a week. I kept hoping that she would make some friends; that this was only temporary.

About a month after I moved in I got a call from an attorney. Joe had filed for divorce, and I became so angry. I just uprooted my whole life, my kids' lives. Why was he doing this?

He said, "I changed my mind, I don't think this is going to work."

"Yeah, right your kids have been at you and have been since the start." I thought.

We hadn't even been living there very long. We hadn't had any problems, so I knew exactly what it was.

I got myself an attorney and then what happened? He changed his mind.

That was a horrible summer. I missed most of it because I didn't go anywhere or do anything except the lake with the kids. I began to feel like a prisoner in my house.

Finally, the weekend before Thanksgiving, I decided I was going to go to the club with my daughter. He told me I couldn't go and I'm like "Uh yes, I'm going." I went, and I had a blast. I stayed the night at my daughter's house. I went home the next day. I had a hangover from hell, but I had fun.

He didn't say anything and was very pleasant. Cool, he must have just accepted it. He didn't mention it. Little did I know he had something in the works. We had Thanksgiving at the house. I invited his family and my family. We had a houseful, and it went off without a hitch. It was great everyone got along. It was an awesome day.

On Monday, I got a phone call from my attorney.

She said, "Joe has refiled."

This was bullshit; I was so angry!

She said, "He didn't say anything to you?"

said," No he hadn't."

He had called his attorney the day before Thanksgiving. He was obviously upset about me going out and the fact that I told him I was going to start spending more time with my kids. I needed to be there more for them because I hadn't been. I knew this and felt really guilty.

Not all of it was Joe's fault. I had become depressed during this time. I didn't want to do anything, so I am partly at fault for not living up to my responsibilities. There was a lot of arguing and drama that went on for the next two months. My kids were very outspoken and rude, and well I wasn't very nice either. It was probably best that we moved out. I didn't want Joe and me to hate each other. What we had was so special. I didn't want it to be destroyed with a lot of bitter memories.

HIS RETURN

I hadn't heard from Blane all weekend. That bummed me out. I was hoping he would call me, but he didn't. It was Tuesday when he called me. The reason I remember the day is because I parked down the street from my favorite client's house waiting for it to be time for me to go clean.

He sounded bummed out and from what he said to me I understand why. He said, "He couldn't see me anymore because he was not allowed to date anyone with minor children because of the trumped-up charges he was convicted."

I said, "Okay and I had fun."

I hung up and texted my daughter and said, "Well, that didn't last long. I really liked him". Oops. I sent that to him. I was so grateful that I hadn't slept with him. I would have felt used, but I didn't have to worry about that.

He texted me and said, "You sent that to the wrong person."

"Oh sorry." I went about my day but was filled with disappointment.

When I got home, Harmony asked me what was wrong. I told her Blane had called. He said he couldn't see me. I said, "It's probably for the best seeing's how he is on the sex offender registry."

That night he called me, and I didn't answer. He kept calling and texting me, telling me to answer the phone.

Finally, I did, and he said, "That we could be friends. They can't stop me from having friends." We were fooling ourselves when we thought we could just be friends. We talked on the phone for a long time that night, and I told him about me having to move and what had been going on.

THE MOVE

The day had finally arrived, and it was time to move. A lot of my stuff had been taken to my house. Today, I was getting what was left. I had a large armoire that Joe had bought for Harmony because there was no closet in her room. It was very large, brown, and had two large drawers, on the side a place to hang clothes and two large shelves. It was not beautiful, but it was nice.

We tried to get to get it up the stairs and when I say we I'm talking four guys. They tried everything, took the doors off, moved it this way and that way, and they just couldn't do it. My brother told me we were just going to have to leave it.

I said, "No", and started to cry. Just then my phone rang and it was Blane. He asked me what was wrong and I told him all about my dilemma with the armoire. He said, he could get it out for me, and I said, "If these guys can't do it why do you think that you can".

He said, "Just give me the address and I guarantee you that I will get it out".

Once he arrived I brought him inside and took him directly downstairs and showed him the armoire and he said, "Oh that's no problem".

He tied a rope around it, tied the rope around himself, and began pulling it up the stairs. I stood there in shock and amazement. All these guys and they couldn't do it and here he was one person, getting it out all by himself. I was so happy. I really didn't want to have to leave it behind.

Later, Blane walked up to Joe who was sitting in his chair and introduced himself and shook his hand.

Everyone was outside waiting for me. I had all of my stuff out and it was time to say goodbye. It was heartbreaking. We gave each other a hug and began to cry. We still cared so much for each other. I told him I loved him. I felt horrible I had promised Joe that I would be there for him to the very end, that I would never leave him but really, he was the one who sent me away.

I walked out through the laundry room to get into my van. Blane was in my van. I began crying again because I was losing my best friend, I didn't care what anyone said or thought. I loved Joe and he had become such an important and intricate part of my life. I felt so empty and sad the rest of that day. I went to Blane's and lay on his couch and fell asleep. I was so exhausted from all the emotions that I had been going through all day.

He had made dinner while I was sleeping and was doing everything he could to lift my spirits. I hadn't told him a whole lot about Joe but he could tell that it was having a huge effect on me.

THE FIRST TIME

Blane called and asked if I would like to come over for dinner, and a movie that evening. I said that would be great.

I arrived around six, and he was in the kitchen cooking. The stereo was blaring with country music. He looked so cute preparing dinner. He smiled at me and said, "Pull up a seat darling." The way he said it just melted my heart. He kept looking at me smiling. I asked him if he wanted me to help and he said, "No I got this."

He asked about my day and listened attentively as I told him about it. That conversation was so long ago I can't remember what happened that particular day. I'm sure it wasn't anything significant because most of my days were pretty much the same. Cleaning someone's house, although there were times when I went to some jobs that put a lasting memory in my head, either because the client is; let's just say some of them can be difficult or wanted me to do something out of the ordinary. But if memory serves me right that was just like any other day.

He had prepared chicken, rice and green beans. I'm so glad it was green beans because I hate vegetables. Green beans are one of the few I like. We sat down to dinner, and he blessed the food.

Ninety percent of the time we would pray over our meals. I liked that because God is very important in my life. It also made me believe that he was a good guy.

After enjoying our dinner. We went and sat on the couch and began to watch a movie that Blane had picked up at Redbox.

We sat close to each other and put our feet up on the coffee table, his hand resting on my thigh. He turned towards me and gently kissed my lips. He placed his hand on the side of my head. I kissed him back.

After kissing for several minutes, He picked me up off the couch and continued to kiss me as he carried me to his bed. He gently placed me on the bed and then lay down next to me.

We continue to make out. He began rubbing me along my side. It felt so wonderful; it had been so long since I had been touched in this way. He slowly removed my blouse, and he began to rub my breasts, he began to suck on my breast as he ran his hands down my thigh and placed his hand between my legs. He slowly entered me, and I melted into ecstasy. I pulled his shirt off and began sucking on his neck. I tried to undo his pants and was not very successful, so he undid them and pulled them off. We began kissing again hard and with a lot of passion. We were both breathing very heavily. He climbed on top of me and slowly entered me.

It hurt at first because it had been such a long time for me and he was well endowed. I felt it when he finally released himself into me. He rolled off of me onto his side and began softly kissing me. Then he got up and went to the bathroom. He came back with a warm washcloth and gently cleaned me up.

He was amazing. He laid back down on the bed next to me and propped himself up with his arm and his hand placed on his head. He told me I was beautiful and how much he enjoyed spending time with me. "I replied that I enjoyed his company as well." We cuddled up close together and fell asleep.

In the night, I felt him sit up. I opened my eyes and then suddenly his fist came crashing down on my chin. He then laid back down on his side and went back to sleep. I lay there with tears streaming down my face. What just happened? I didn't understand.

The next morning, I asked him what happened, and he didn't know what I was talking about. He said that he was dreaming that he caught his brother and me together and that he hit his brother. He told me how every woman he had ever been with had cheated on him, that he had major trust issues because of that. He hugged me and said he was so sorry, that he would never do anything like that to hurt me intentionally. He seemed very remorseful.

I believed him about not knowing what he did while he was asleep because my son would sleepwalk a lot when he was younger. One time I found him sleeping on the front porch and when I asked why. He said he did not remember how he got there.

ROAD TRIP

We started spending a lot of time together and would talk on the phone several times throughout the day. One weekend he had to go to Richfield to work on a job his Dad had contracted. It had been awhile since he had worked on it because they had to wait for the weather to get better and the snow to melt. He called me and asked if I could pick up some supplies that they needed and deliver them. I said, "Sure." He told me what I needed and were to go to get them.

On the drive, out I had very bad gas. I was so bored just driving; it was a long drive. I began to entertain myself by coming up with an acronym for the word fart. I couldn't stop farting so I came up with Forced Air Rectally Transmitted. I began to laugh at myself. I got lost finding the place which is something I do quite a lot when it's dark. I can't see very well in the dark. I have night blindness, and that makes it difficult.

I finally found the place. It was very late. I hadn't had time to shower before leaving Salt Lake, so I decided to take a bath. He came in and sat on the toilet and talked to me about the project they were working on. Boring. I didn't care because it's not my thing, but I listened and acted interested.

He began to wash my back. I then got out, and he helped me dry off. I put the same clothes back on because I hadn't planned on staying. It was very late, and I was tired. There was no way I could make the drive home safely.

His cousin Marty was there, so I had to sleep in my clothes. Marty was a very nice guy. He was always cracking jokes. He was very tall, long blond hair, pretty blue eyes. He made me laugh.

We got up the next morning and had breakfast at the hotel. They served a free continental breakfast with the room. They chowed down, and I just ate a little. I wasn't very hungry. Blane asked me if I could stay and go work on the job with them. I didn't have any other plans for the weekend, and I figured the kids would be okay without me.

Once we arrived at the job site, Blane assigned me a job of untangling some string that they needed to measure between the holes they had dug. I didn't know any better so; I spent like what seemed forever untangling the string.

He then asked me to move these huge cardboard type tubes to the other side of the site. He said, "They can't touch the ground." I struggled to get them over to the other side and made sure they didn't hit the ground. Marty and Blane began laughing hysterically. There was still one left for me to move and Blane began to roll it over. He was pulling my chain when he said they couldn't touch the ground. Then two of them thought they were so funny. I guess I should have known, seeing how they were going into the ground. I felt like an idiot but just told them, "Your jerks," and laughed with them. All in all, it, was a good day.

Blane asked if I would like to stay again that night and look at some other potential jobs. Marty headed back to Salt Lake; we headed south.

We drove up to Brian Head to just go sightseeing. It was beautiful, and I thought to myself, I would love to come here for a weekend and bring my kids. We all love to snowboard, even though none of us are very good.

We had fun when we do go. We had to go shopping so that I could buy me some clothes. I needed to get out of the clothes I was wearing because they were dirty from the hard day of work, and I had been wearing them the day before. I also bought him a few shirts that were on sale. They were nice Pendletons, and for the price, I couldn't pass them up.

After we had looked at a few job sites, we ended up in Fillmore. We got a hotel and decided to get something to eat.

As we drove past the jail, Blane told me that he had spent some of his time there. He told me about how he worked on the forest crew and would cut the trees, remove garbage, and do anything to the trails to make them accessible to the public. He said that being able to go outside and do that made his time in there bearable.

We bought dinner from Costa Vida and took it back to the motel room. We walked into the room, and it was freezing. We had turned on the heater before we left so it should have been warm by the time we returned.

I went to the manager's office, and they said they would call someone to fix it. I said that was ok we would just like a refund. We were tired after the long day of working and driving around and didn't feel like waiting. They gave me a partial refund, and I told them that was bullshit and wanted all of my money back. I didn't get it and just decided it wasn't worth the fight. I was too tired.

We went down the street to a different hotel, which was much nicer than the previous one. We got our room and finally got to eat our dinner. By this time, it was cold, but I was so hungry I didn't care.

We decided to take a shower. He began washing my hair. He took the body wash and spread it all over my body. He was so gentle; he made me feel like a princess, telling me how soft my skin was, that I was beautiful, how happy he was that he met me.

We began to kiss each other rubbing our bodies against each other we made our way out of the shower and to the bed. We fell onto the bed, kissing each other passionately. He climbed on top of me and entered me. We moved together in unison it felt so perfect. We changed positions several times each one bringing a different sense of pleasure.

We lay back on the bed, and he said, "That was amazing."

I couldn't agree more. It was; well words can't express the feeling.

We began playing around, and he would pull the hair on my leg and tease me because I hadn't shaved for quite a while and I had a small forest growing. "Oh yeah," I said and began pulling the hair on his arms. We were having such a great time. He told me to stop several times; I didn't. He became angry in a flash and slapped my thigh hard. I froze tears began to well up in my eyes.

"I told you to stop." he said.

I suddenly felt like a little girl that had just gotten in trouble. I got up and went into the bathroom. I didn't want him to see my cry. I went back into the room and climbed onto the bed, and he grabbed me and pulled me close to him as he continued to watch TV. He fell asleep, and I just laid there looking at the ceiling.

I felt numb.

We had breakfast at the restaurant that was connected to the hotel. I barely ate anything. I was trying to figure out what to do. Nothing was said about what happened the night before. It was as if it didn't happen.

We had a few more stops to make and then back off to Salt Lake. The drive home was very quiet. I didn't have much to say and just listened to the music.

He commented that I was awfully quiet, I usually talk a mile a minute about this and that. He said he loved that about me, that I was always rambling on about something. I think I do that when I'm nervous.

VALENTINES DAY

I love holidays and tend to go overboard. I was so excited about Valentine's day this year because I had fallen in love with Blane. I wanted this to be special. I found a beautiful red plate with jewels that went around the outer rim and a cute Valentine cup that I filled with Kisses.

I decided to make fudge in heart-shaped molds, as I have been told that I make the best fudge. I have a client who asks me every year at Christmas if I'm going to be making it.

I spent the day looking forward to giving it to him that evening. I also bought chocolate shaped hearts to put on the plate.

I waited for him to call. When I hadn't heard from him, I began calling him and texting him. I was getting upset and irritated. My feelings were so hurt. Why was he not calling or texting me back? I was upset and decided to go to bed.

Then he called about eleven and said he had been working on a friend's car and had lost track of time and his phone was upstairs on the charger. He was so sorry and asked me to come over. I told him no. My feelings were really hurt. He sounded disappointed that I wasn't going to come over, but I didn't care.

The next day he asked me over for dinner, and I went. I gave him what I had made, and he said, "Oh how sweet. Thank you, honey, I love you".

Oh, my God, he said he loved me, I immediately forgave him for yesterday.

He gave me a box of candy and said, "I saw this and thought of you." It had a picture of a dog on it. I love dogs, and he knew that. So, I let the past go and just brushed it off. Besides, he was helping somebody with their car, and that was a really nice thing to do. It would be selfish of me not to want him to help.

We enjoyed dinner together and watched a movie. We went to bed and began to kiss ever so softly. He ran his hands through my hair, and gently caressed my body. I rubbed my hands along his back. He slowly moved down and placed his head between my thighs and began to nibble on my thighs as he rubbed my leg. He gently placed his mouth on my vagina and began softly licking it, slowly he lifted himself and came up to me, looked me in the eye, and said, "I love you." Then began to kiss my neck while he entered me. He seemed to put so much care into making sure I felt good. I reciprocated because I had fallen in love with him.

We went late into the night. He seemed to be able to last forever. I spent the night, and to my amazement, he wanted more. I was so sore, but because I loved him, I didn't turn him down.

We had coffee, a quick shower and off to work I went. I would go to his house every morning for coffee after I would wake the kids. I started spending more and more time at his house. We made love every day. We couldn't get enough of each other.

MELTING POT

It was my son James birthday. Blane and I asked him and his girlfriend out to dinner to celebrate. I have always taken my kids to dinner for their birthday. I always let them choose where they wanted to go. This year was no different. James had decided we should go somewhere we had never been before, and I thought that was an excellent idea. Blane and I got there a little early, and they were running late.

As we sat in the waiting area, Blane got a phone call. He looked at it and went to put it away.

I said, "Why don't you answer it? Who was it"?

He proceeded to tell me it was a girl he met on POF (the same dating site he met me on) and she just wouldn't quit calling him. I asked him if he had told her he had a girlfriend,

"Yes, but she just keeps calling, and I just don't answer. She'll give up eventually".

Then, James and Kennedy walked up, and we were immediately seated. We couldn't understand at first how things were done because it was not a typical type of dining. We talked to our server who explained it all to us. It was very different. I'm a very picky eater so, there were some things that just didn't appeal to me. Now the desserts, that is a different story. I love the sweet stuff. I have the worst eating habits and prefer junk food to regular healthy stuff.

I don't remember much of what we talked about that evening; I was too busy wondering if he was working on someone's car on Valentine's Day or was he with that girl. I kept those thoughts to myself because I didn't want to seem like the jealous, insecure girlfriend.

When the bill arrived, I went into shock. I could not believe what it had cost. Everyone looked at it and couldn't believe it, but that is the price you pay for fine dining. James and I talked about the dinner we had gone to on mine and Kennedy's birthday, and how the same thing had happened.

We all walked outside together, and I gave them both a hug and told them I loved them. I make it a point to tell my kids I love them every chance I can, every time I talk to them on my phone. I want them to know, and if it's the last time I talk to or see them I want them to remember that "The last thing mom said to me was she loved me."

CARS FOR SALE

We were driving past a vehicle impound yard one day, and Blane told me that some cars that get impounded and unclaimed, were seized. They auctioned them off to the highest bidder. He said some of them were wrecked, and others were perfectly fine. He said we should purchase some, fix them, and sell them. He knew that I had the money to do it. I told him about the settlement I got in the divorce. He said we could make quick, easy money. It sounded like a good idea.

Bidding on the cars, was so much fun. We would work together as a team cleaning them up. We found lots of stuff in the cars, clothes, tools, movies, toys, and a lot of other miscellaneous items.

I would watch him as he repaired them and fetched the tools he would need. We sold a few and made some money. We had a Subaru that was parked out in front of the shop. We got a call on it one day. They asked a lot of questions, things that they really shouldn't have asked if they were just looking to buy the car.

I hurried and got off the phone and then called the number back. It was the parole office that had called. I was scared. We weren't supposed to be having a relationship because of Blane's parole stipulations. I called Blane immediately and let him know about the call.

He said, "Just remember we are only friends and nothing more."

I was always worried that they were going to show up when I was at his house. I had counted the steps on the stairs countless times, thinking and planning my escape if they showed up. I lived with that fear for 11 months always wondering and worrying if this is going to be the day.

Then finally that day came. I was upstairs sleeping in his bed when I heard him say, "Julee."

I sat up and there stood his parole officer and his partner. Thank God, I was dressed. Usually, I would have nothing on because I hated the restraint of clothes and sometimes it would get very hot when he had the furnace running. I looked at them and I said, "Hi my name is Julee and Blane is working on my daughter's car." Luckily that is exactly what he was doing.

They asked him if there was anything more to the story and he straight up lied and said, "No sir. I know that it would be against my parole to date her because she has minor children". They apparently believed him because we heard nothing more.

We continued to sell the cars. On one of the days when we went to the impound lot to purchase cars, we noticed that we were being watched. Blane said he looked like AP&P. I immediately jumped into action and put my arm around his brother and gave him a peck on the lips. I acted like I was his girlfriend the whole time we were there calling him honey and sticking close to his side. I'm very good at acting. I learned as a child how to act in many of the situations I encountered. Hiding my feelings and putting on a show is something that is required if you want to survive. I learned I had to do whatever is necessary sometimes to get by.

If you had been there that day, you would've thought Dale was my boyfriend and not Blane. I watched the PO (PAROLE OFFICER) out of the corner of my eye. He eventually left, and nothing ever came of it. So, I assume he bought my act. I thought for sure that Blane was going to say something to me about kissing Dale. He didn't he understood that I did what was necessary to keep us from getting caught.

THE WARNING

My nephew, Wyatt, called me and said he would like to see me, that he needed to talk to me, and asked me if I had time to meet him for coffee. We made plans to meet at a coffee shop in Sandy near his house. It was a large coffee shop, and it had a stage.

He brought his daughter with him; she was so cute. She said, "Daddy would you dance with me?"

He is such a great and loving Dad that he said, "Yes honey I will dance with you."

It didn't matter to him that the coffee shop was full of people. He got up there on that stage and danced with his little princess. I was smiling from ear to ear just watching him. Such a wonderful father that has gone to great lengths to be in her life. After he came and sat with me at the table, and his little girl stayed on the stage twirling around.

He said, "Julee, I'm very concerned about this guy you're seeing. I have talked to some people, and he is not a good guy.

I told him, Blane told me about the charges and he said they weren't true. He was also very concerned about us buying and selling cars. He felt that he was taking advantage of me.

I assured him that I was all right and I knew what I was doing.

My nephew has always been an important person in my life. He was my real live baby doll when I was a little girl. I would change him, feed him, and treat him like he was my own. It made me feel good to know that he loved me enough to talk to me and warn me. But it was too late. I was in love and was now blinded by it.

I look back now, and wish I would have listened to him, and escaped the hell I was about to live. As I drove home from our meeting, I started thinking about our conversation and wondered who it was that had talked to him. I started thinking maybe I should look into things. I began asking Blane questions about his charges, and he would try to avoid answering. Although one time he did comment that the girl's hymens hadn't been broken. So how could they charge him? They had no concrete evidence, and he also said, "You see how large I am I would have broken them in two if I had raped them."

GIRLS? I thought he had been accused of one girl, one time. That set off an alarm in my head I needed to go find out exactly why he had spent 13 years in prison. I decided that I needed to go to the court house and see what was there.

I went to the courthouse and gave them his name. I stood there for what seemed like forever, waiting for the clerk to bring me his file. She handed me the file. It was very thick, and I thought, "Wow I'm going to be here for a while."

I pulled up a chair and sat at the desk and began to go through it. First, I looked at all the charges. There were a lot of drug possession charges, domestic violence and multiple counts of sodomy on a minor. I couldn't find any court proceedings on some of the accusations. I asked the court clerk why this was, and she said after so long they don't keep them.

The information I came for was there in black and white right in front of my face. I began reading and began to get sick to my stomach. Two little girls nine and twelve. I couldn't find any medical reports in the file, only their testimony and what he said. He didn't take it to trial. He plea bargained instead, to lesser charges.

The things that they said he did made my heart ache. Oh, my God, I had fallen in love with a monster. How could anyone do what he had done to those girls?

I cried all the way home. What was I going to do? I was in love with him. He didn't seem like the person in that file.

I hadn't seen any sign of him being that way. My nephew had warned me, the people who talked to him must have known, but I didn't want to believe it. I began to ask him more about his charges, and he would get irritated, and I finally blurted out that I had gone to the courthouse and read his file.

He looked at me and said, "So? It was all lies." It didn't seem to bother him at all.

What do you want to know? "Did I, do it? No, like I told you, my ex was pissed at me and fed those girls all that info, and I asked why then did the girls get so upset when the therapist talked to them, and he said, "I spanked them when they misbehaved."

I wouldn't let them get away with all the things their mother did, and they hated me for that." Again, he referenced the size of his penis and how it was impossible to do the things he was accused of. He went on and talked about his other ex. The mother of his two girls and said that it all started because of her. She had made accusations about his girl's, she hid them from him and wouldn't let him see them, and that is where the mother of the little girls got the idea to try and set him up. He was married to the mother of the two little girls which made him their stepfather. He had an answer for everything. So, I just let it go. Although I would watch his behavior always looking for signs, why I didn't know what was I going to do.

When he talked about his kids, he would get very sad, he told me how his oldest was his sidekick, and they had spent a lot of time together. He was very angry about the fact that his ex-girlfriend kept them from him. That it was not fair, he was a good Dad and would do anything for them. He said, "She cheated on him, as a matter of fact, he said every woman he had ever been with had cheated."

Hmmmmm, he was probably the cheater.

She was just vindictive because I was with someone else. Blane, painted her out to be a monster. He was the victim! At least that is how he portrayed everything.

His oldest daughter wanted nothing to do with him. He kept trying to build a relationship with her, and she would have none of that.

His youngest daughter who was in her 20's, would talk to him on the phone. She came by the shop a few times. She came over on Easter Sunday for a quick visit, and we took some pictures. She was a very sweet girl. Her hubby was deployed. When he came back, they had a get together at a pizza parlor. We really shouldn't have been there because there were a couple of minors. Part of his parole stipulations was to not have any contact with children without it being preapproved. He didn't care he was always breaking the rules. I was extremely uncomfortable because Blane had dated his mother-in-law. Yeah, he shit, in his own backyard at least that's what I think. So here I am hanging out with his ex. I didn't let it show that it bothered me. I just smiled, ate, and enjoyed myself.

On the way home, I razzed him about her. I told him she wasn't very pretty. I asked, "Why does she hold her hand over her mouth when she talks and when she eats? Is she toothless or does she have rotten teeth?" He said, "He didn't know why she did it. She had teeth." It wouldn't be the last event that I had to be in her presence.

He had mentioned on many occasions how nice it would be to have a boat. We would see a boat, and he made comments on how wonderful it would be to float on the lake and fish. After we had left his son-in-law's homecoming, I said, "Why don't we stop by the boat shop and look around."

I had a boat once, and I knew how much fun and enjoyable it could be, although when I owned my other boat, I only had a few good times because my ex-husband had a way of destroying many of our boat outings. Have I mentioned that he was a real winner too? NOT. We walked around and climbed on several boats. Then we saw her. She was beautiful, red and white, 23 feet long, and in pristine condition. We both fell in love with her. I was able to sign for the boat with nothing down. I had impeccable credit. That hasn't always been the case.

When I married my ex-husband the father of my two youngest, I had good credit, and it was destroyed when we divorced. My life with my ex is another story in its self, something that needs to be told as we'll, but not now. We took the boat that very day.

I called the kids to tell them I had a surprise. We showed up to the house to show them the new boat. At first, Harmony was excited, and then Blane said something. I don't know what but it sent her into a rage. She began yelling hurtful things at him. Then she was yelling at me. What she was really angry about was that I had been spending more time with him than I was with them. She had every right to be angry, and I had been spending was too much time at his house.

We took the boat over to his place. I told him I needed to go home and spend some time with the kids. I went home. Harmony was in her room with the boy she was seeing. Bennett was playing at his friend's house down the street. I asked them if they wanted to watch a movie and they said, "Yes."

As we were watching the movie, he began texting me. I told him we were watching a movie. Then he called me. Harmony flew into a rage. "He never lets you be with us. We can't even watch a movie without him interrupting". She stormed off to her room. I tried to get her to come out, but she refused. Bennett said, "I've never even met him, and I hate him."

I gave up and went out to my room and went to bed. The next morning in the kitchen Harmony said, "Bennett do you want to know why you haven't met Blane?"

He said, "Yes."

Harmony said, "Because he is a pedophile and likes to rape little girls." He looked at me, and I said, "He had been charged with that, but I don't believe he did it. He can't be around minors, and that is why he has had to stay away from you kids."

I was angry at Harmony for telling him. I wanted to be the one to tell him. At least now he knew it wasn't that he didn't want to know him, but that he couldn't.

I LOVED SUNDAYS

We went to church at Calvary. One Sunday morning as I was putting on my makeup for church. Blane came into the bathroom. He told me he didn't know why I put makeup on. I was beautiful without it. I took it as a compliment. I said it makes me feel better about myself and gives me confidence. I continued to put it on. He said that to me many times.

It started to feel like he was not complimenting me. He didn't want me to wear it. It wasn't like I wore it all the time only on special occasions, and church. He began giving me a disapproving look when I would wear it. I eventually stopped wearing it all together.

At Church, I felt like I was home. We would get there early to eat breakfast. They always made the best food. The only thing I didn't like about go to the breakfast was that it was located right next to the children's ministry. There were constantly children in our presence. I would watch Blane out of the corner of my eye. He was avoiding looking at them as if he was afraid to look at them. It was weird.

After we would eat, we would go right into the sanctuary. We always sat towards the back on the left side. Blane said, "That when he came with Sophia, they would sit on the other side. Except she made him sit behind her, and walk behind her because she didn't want anyone to know they were together." They also hid their relationship from his daughter because she was her mother-in-law.

I loved to sing and always enjoyed the worship time. When Blane would sing, I would just look at him and smile trying with all my might not to laugh. He sounded like a wounded animal that needed to be put out of its misery. I wasn't going to say anything to take away his joy.

Our pastor always had great messages. He kept you interested and at times could get the whole congregation laughing. I had been going to that church since November 2006. I had some friends there. I introduced Blane to them. Something, Sophia wouldn't do. I didn't want him to think that I was ashamed of being seen with him.

After Church, every other Sunday I would go out to my mom and Dads. I did Dad's grocery shopping because neither of them was in good enough health to do it. Blane went to the store with me a few times. Then he started staying at the house with Dad. My parents loved him. They thought that I had finally picked a winner. I hadn't told them about his past. I figured that I would eventually. After grocery shopping was done, we would play Yahtzee. Dad loved YAHTZEE.

We would play for hours. When Dad got a YAHTZEE, it was awesome he would get so excited. He'd smile from ear to ear and practically come out of his chair. It would make me laugh. Blane and I would goof around and play. We would have so much fun.

Mom stayed upstairs while we played. Her hands aren't that great so she would just watch her TV shows. We would go upstairs and visit mom after we got our butts kicked by Dad. Blane was always helping with the yard and anything else my Dad needed. He seemed like such an awesome man.

TIFFANY

One afternoon, a few weeks after Easter, I was at home taking a nap. My kids came in my room super excited. Harmony and Tatiana said in unison, "My friend has a Chihuahua that she is selling." Harmony asked if we could buy her.

I said, "No I don't want any more dogs."

They left and returned a short time later. They had brought the puppy back with them. They placed her in my hands. It was all over. I was in love. She was so tiny she fit in the palm of my hand, soft fuzzy red hair, and the cutest little eyes. I had to have her. I asked the girl how much they wanted for her.

She said, "Two hundred dollars." I said, "I have one hundred here and need to go to the bank to get the other hundred."

She said, "Okay."

I took the puppy with me to go to the bank. I decided to take her over to Blane's' house to show him.

I got there, and Blane and my oldest daughter Ali were standing outside next to her Jeep. He had been working on it for her. I said, "Blane look at my new puppy. Isn't she beautiful?"

He said, "You need to take it back. You have enough on your plate. The last thing you need is another dog".

I said, "I can't."

He said, "Why"?

I said, "Because I love her."

He asked, "How can you love her? You just got her."

I said, "It was love at first sight."

He shook his head and walked away. He said, "Whatever! Do what you want."

I did exactly that. I kept her. That night we tossed around names. We ended up agreeing on Tiffany. We also call her tippy, tiff tiff, and I sometimes would call her tippy toes. Blane's Dad calls her poopers.

That night I laid her next to me in the bed. She climbed under the covers and climbed between my legs and curled into a little ball and went sound asleep. She decided that is where she likes to sleep, and that is where she still sleeps to this day.

We went to Walmart the next day. I was getting Tiffany some dog food. Blane headed straight for the dog toys. I asked, "What are you doing? You didn't even want me to keep her."

He replied, "She needs toys to play with."

He fell in love with her just like I did. We both love her so much.

She has run away a couple of times. I don't think she meant to. She just gets curious and goes too far. One time when she did that, and I couldn't find her I cried myself to sleep.

The next morning, I was sitting on the porch crying when my phone rang. Someone had found her and called the number on her chip tag. I started crying even harder because I was so happy that someone had found my baby.

Blane's Dad told us we could not have her at the apartment. Blane never goes by rules. He told me just make sure if she has an accident you clean it up, so Dad doesn't know we have her here. We got her trained when she got a little bigger to go up and down the stairs. She would go potty outside and sometimes she would go somewhere down in the shop. She was a real comfort to me. I would hold onto her and cry when things got bad.

ANSWER THE PHONE

Sometimes when I'm working, I don't hear my phone. Blane started asking me why I didn't answer it in an accusing way. He then started telling me that I wasn't at work. I would say I was vacuuming or whatever it was, but he would say, "Yea right." I tried to make sure to answer when he called because I didn't want to fight.

One day my phone rang, and I thought for sure it was Blane. I hurried and got it out of my pocket. It wasn't Blane. It was Joe. I hurried and answered it.

Joe said, "Hi honey. I miss you. I Love. Can we have lunch or dinner sometime."

I replied, "Yes, how about lunch Friday, I will be at your house at two."

"That would be great," He replied.

I didn't tell Blane because I didn't want him to stop me from seeing Joe. I had thought a lot about him but was afraid to call him. I was afraid of him not wanting to talk to me. It would have hurt because I still cared about him.

I meet with Joe for lunch that Friday and he said, "I missed you so much." He wished he hadn't had let me go.

I said, "I've missed you too."

Joe said, "Julee I honestly wanted you to have my house. I'm so sorry. In place of that, I want to pay off your house."

I replied, "Joe you don't have to do that. You have already given me more than I deserve."

Joe said, "I have been thinking about this for quite some time, and I want to do it. I love you, and I want to know that you are going to be okay when I'm gone. You have to promise me one thing. That you won't take any money out against the house, it needs to stay paid off so when the time comes when you can't continue to work the way you do you will have a home."

With tears in my eyes, I replied, "I don't know what to say. I'm overwhelmed. Thank you."

Joe said, "Can you be at my house Monday morning with your house paperwork?"

"Yes," I replied.

We finished our lunch. We went back to Joe's house, and I stayed for a couple of hours watching TV. We talked about how things were with his family, and I told him about work and the kids. I didn't mention anything about Blane.

That night I told Blane that I had seen Joe. He got quiet and just looked at me. He was pissed. I went on to tell him what Joe wanted to do for me. He said, "That's great. Good for you."

I said, "Joe means a lot to me. I'm going to talk to him."

He replied, "Whatever." That was the end of that for the time being.

Blane started going out of town a lot more. I was glad because it gave me a chance to spend time at home with the kids. Except now the kids didn't want to spend time with me. They were angry. They also would rather be with their friends. I also liked it when he was gone because I had time to rest.

He wanted sex constantly. He began having a hard time staying hard. He claimed it was probably because he jacked off so much when he was in jail. That didn't stop him from trying. He would keep going. Trying to make it work. I would ask him to stop. He wouldn't. He would just keep going. It began to burn and hurt. I would just squeeze my eyes shut and hope he would just give up.

I began to pay attention to when it was occurring. I also began to notice that Blane was getting phone calls from the girl that called him back in February. When I would say anything to him, he would get defensive and say, "You are probably the one who is cheating. I spend all my time with you except when I have to go to work. You are so insecure. You need to get over it, or this just isn't going to work."

I would then feel like I was insecure. I already had low self-esteem and him not being able to perform made me feel like maybe it was me.

One morning as I was getting ready to leave for work he said, "Where do you think you're going?"

I said, "To work."

Blane said, "Not yet. You need to take care of me first."

I said, "I have to go. I'm going to be late."

He reached out and grabbed my red sweat pants and dragged me over to him. I struggled and tried to fight him. He was to strong. He was sitting in the yellow dining room chair. He pulled my sweat pants down. He had already removed his penis from his pants. He spits on his penis and pulled me back and placed me on it and then pushed it up inside of me. It hurt like hell. He held on to my thighs and lifted me up and down until he was spent. I walked into the bathroom and cleaned up. I just walked down the stairs tears began streaming down my face.

I got in my car and left. He called and said, "I love you honey have a great day." Wow. He doesn't feel like he did anything wrong. How could he not know how bad he just hurt me. How can he not know that all the times I ask him to stop or tell him he's hurting me that it's causing me harm? I don't know why I didn't just leave. I don't know what was wrong with me.

It started happening all the time. The showers that I loved at first became a nightmare. I would sometimes shower before he got home. He would then accuse me off having to clean up. I had been with someone else. I stopped showering until he got home even though I knew what I would have to endure.

What is wrong with me? Why the hell did I stay? I could no longer deny it to myself, that he did do all those things to those two little girls. I wondered if there were others.

I tried to break it off with him several times. He would start calling me, texting, and he even showed up to my house. I would always fall back in. I began hating myself. I didn't care about anything. I just went through the days like a robot. I couldn't tell anyone. I was ashamed and felt worthless. I didn't want anyone to know.

TAKING MY PARENTS CAMPING

Dad had made several comments about wanting to go fishing. We decided it would be great to take mom and Dad camping. They both loved camping and hadn't gone in years. We made reservations for Yuba Lake. We got a site that was away from the camp grounds because Blane was not allowed to be in the campsites.

Upon arriving, we realized there was no way to keep Dad's oxygen going because there were no electrical hook ups. We ended up having to stay in the campsites. Blane didn't seem concerned. He figured they wouldn't find out because he was so far away from Salt Lake.

We set up our camp. Blane and I put our tent up together. We couldn't decide which way to put the door, so it took us a few because we kept switching it around. Mom and Dad stayed in their camper. It was really nice to see them enjoying themselves.

We went out on the boat the next day. It was a little cramped because we had to bring Dad's port a potty. He suffered from Crohn's disease and when he had to go. He had to go.

We fished most of the day. Nobody caught anything. That really didn't matter. It was just about being out there together enjoying ourselves.

When we got back to shore we began making dinner; we'll I was making dinner. I got everything prepared, then served mom and Dad their food. I was just getting ready to sit down with my plate, and Dad asked me to feed the dog.

I said, "Dad, I'm going to sit down and eat my dinner. Your dog can wait until I'm done."

I sat down and ate my dinner. I then fed his dog. That was something I never did. I always did what Dad asked as soon as he asked. I finally stood up for myself. He was a little shocked when I did it. I had just had enough of jumping every time he barked an order at me.

Blane and I went into town to pick up some things from the store. We saw some wave runners on the side of the road with a for sale sign on them. We stopped and looked at them. They were in excellent condition, and they were a good price. We decided to call and check it out with the owner. We made plans to meet with him the next day to test them. We met the guy who just happened to be a Bishop at a small lake near his home. We loved them, and I decided to buy them. I thought the kids would really enjoy them. We had planned a trip for the next weekend to go pick them up.

That night Blane wanted to have sex. I said, "I don't want to." He didn't listen and kept rubbing on me. I would say stop. But he didn't. He eventually climbed on top of me. I just laid there and let him do what he wanted. I would just go somewhere else in my head.

The next morning, I got up and went on as usual. I didn't want my parents to know what was going on. They liked Blane, and I didn't want to disappoint them.

We went out on the lake for a short time, after which we went back to camp and started cleaning everything up.

Blane asked me why I was so quiet on the trip home. I just glared at him. He acted like nothing had happened. Again, I think he believes that what he did was not wrong. On several occasions, he had commented that my body was his and he could do what he wanted. I would say, "I don't think so."

He would say, "I do." Then just go on with whatever it was he was doing.

THE RESEMBLENCE

One evening in early summer, we were relaxing at his apartment. I was sitting in the tan recliner enjoying the massage that the chair was providing. Blane sat across the room on the couch. He was going through the stack of receipts that had accumulated on the coffee table. The lighting was very dim. I looked over at him. I froze. I couldn't believe what I was seeing.

There had been several other times that he reminded me of Brett. One day as I was napping in his bed, he came to the bed with an ice cube and began rubbing it on me while I was sleeping. Of course, it woke me up in a quickness. He then inserted it into me. He thought it was funny. I started yelling at him and he just laughed. He then climbed on me and inserted his penis. He continued until his needs were fulfilled.

On a hot summer day, back in 1982 Brett had come to the bedroom where I was napping. He had a big stick popsicle. He began to rub it on my body and then inserted the popsicle. He removed it and tossed it on the floor. Our little puppy bandit started eating it. Brett climbed on top of me and did his business.

I told my daughter Alisha about how he reminded me of her Dad in many ways. I didn't tell her all the details just that he was a lot like him.

I have a lot of unhealed wounds from my relationship with Brett. He was ripped out of my life in 1984 when he was murdered. There is a lot to be told about that relationship and his murder.

COUNTRY WESTERN CONCERT

It was the first year that the state was putting on a concert that was comparable to the country fest they had in Colorado. There was going to be a lot of very famous bands playing. I bought tickets for the three-day event. We didn't think it would be a good idea to camp at the event and decided we would just drive back and forth. It was only a thirty-minute drive, so it was not a big deal.

The Friday show was okay. We walked around a lot and had dinner. On Saturday, Blane wanted to see a friend that had just got a house in Tooele. He had done time with him in prison. We went to his house, and the guy showed us around.

He asked Blane about a few things he wanted to change and how he would go about doing it.

When we left, we decided to get something to eat. We had found out last night how expensive the food was at the concert. We went to a KFC/TACO BELL. We ordered our food. I ordered a baby lemon cake.

He looked at me and said, "Do you really think you need one of those." It wasn't a question; it was a statement. It was just another way for him to make me feel bad about myself. Like the day, I was going up the stairs at his apartment, and he put his hands on my butt and said, "You know if you go up and down the stairs, it will tighten this up."

I told the guy never mind on the cake. I only ate part of my lunch. I really didn't want to eat any of it, but I knew that would just start a fight. I had been waiting too long for this concert, and I wasn't going to let him ruin it by fighting all day. Besides, I had grown used to his put downs and just let it roll off my back. At least I thought. They were really just storing up.

At the Concert, he was texting all day. He said he was texting his sister Cinnamon. I found out later that wasn't true. He was texting Jill. The girl who kept calling him.

My favorite client Jan, called me to schedule her next cleaning. I hadn't told her that I was dating anyone. She has seen me get hurt too many times over the years, and I didn't want her to see it happen again. I have been working for her since 1993. Blane knew I hadn't told her about him because I would tell him not to call me when I was working for her. He pressured me that day and said I need to tell her about him. I said, "No."

He started saying, "I was ashamed of him. I really wasn't at her house at those times. I was somewhere else. Etc."

So, I told her about him. I wish I had stuck to my guns. She eventually saw me fall apart because of our relationship.

He wore a baseball hat all day because there was a lot of people and he didn't want to take the risk of being recognized. He hadn't asked permission from his parole officer to go to this event. He knew if he had been seen there he would be in trouble.

We met some really nice people that day. I really didn't say much. I just sat there. He talked to them about his construction company. I thought to myself you mean your Dad's, you just work for him for pennies. Which was true his Dad was way cheap. All he ever thought about was his money.

They had made a plan to meet up the next day and sit together again.

He suggested that we buy the kids tickets for the next day and bring them with us. I bought them tickets, but we decided to come in different cars.

Blane thought it would be best if we didn't all sit together. We sat about ten feet behind him and his new friends. Hmm, I think he had this all planned out. I felt like he wanted to not have me with him and that's why he had me bring the kids. Oh, he's good.

Funny thing is the one girl started calling him. He said, "I'm going to be doing some work on her house." He never did do any work on her house.

Although he did do work on one of the other lady's homes, which turned out to be a real mess for him and his Dad. She was very picky. He screwed up her tile work. He had to fix a lot of things. To top it off he didn't complete the job.

When it got dark that night at the concert, a beautiful love song came on. Me and the kids were standing on the walkway watching the show. Blane came up to me and began slow dancing with me. He wreaked like alcohol. He had been drinking all day with his new friends. He swung me around and then pulled me close. He started singing in my ear. I laughed. On the inside of course. I didn't want to upset him.

I was really concerned when the concert was over, and it was time to leave. Blane had been drinking all day and was drunk. I was worried about him driving home. When I said something, he just brushed me off.

When I got home, I called him several times; he didn't answer, and I became more concerned. I decided to drive over to his apartment to see if he had made it home.

I walked upstairs and found him sitting on his couch. I said, "Why didn't you answer your phone."

He said, "I knew you would come over if I didn't." He said that with a smile on his face.

I said, "Looks like you made it home just fine. I'm going home."

Just then he reached out and grabbed my arm. He pulled me down on to the couch. He began kissing me. His breathe was rancid. I turned my head away.

I said, "Stop, let me go. I want to go home." I said it several times, but he just continued. I couldn't move because I was wedged into the back of the couch. I hated that couch. You can't get off of it. It sucks you in and then your trapped.

I closed my eyes, and suddenly I was back in the summer of 1969. I was almost five. Shelly and I were playing at the park across the street from our house. We lived next store to each other. Our moms were best friends. We were also best friends. We were inseparable. We played at the park all the time. The elementary school was connected to the park.

That day we were playing on the merry go round when two older girls approached us. They asked us our names, and if we were their alone. We told them that we were. The tall black girl asked us if we wanted to play, follow the leader.

We said, "Yes." We were excited.

No one ever wanted to play with us. So, we were eager to play.

The black girl said, "Let's split up. I'll take Julee, and you take Shelly". The black girl said, "Follow me." So, I did.

She led me across the field to the school. She had me follow her to a place between two buildings. She turned around and said in a very mean voice, "Take your clothes off." I just stood there. She said it again and grabbed me by the arm. I started taking my clothes slowly. She said, "Hurry up." So, I did.

She was taking her pants off. After my clothes had been off, she told me to lay on the ground. Once I was laying on the ground, she laid on top of me. She smelled. She was breathing hard into my face. She started moving forwards and backward. She started going up and down. I just laid there with tears running down my cheeks. Why was she doing this to me? It seemed like it went on for hours.

I could hear Shelly and the White girl laughing. The white girl was telling Shelly to through it harder. She had Shelly throwing rocks at the school windows.

Then the white girl yelled at her friend, hurry up we got to go. She stood up and told make to get dressed.

Shelly had told the white girl that it was her brother's birthday and that they were going to come looking for us if we didn't come home.

Once I was back with Shelly, we just looked at each other. She knew what was happening to me, but she was only four what could she have done. We never spoke of it after that day. I didn't tell anyone.

When I was in my early twenties, I was in a treatment program. My therapist told me that I had to tell my mom. I didn't want to because I knew my mom would react badly.

I told her, and she called me a liar. She said I was just saying that to get attention. I told her to talk to Shelly. Shelly and I hadn't talked in years. She got ahold of Mrs. Talker Shelly's mom. After talking to them, she came back to see me the next week. She apologized for not believing me. She asked me why I didn't say anything. I just bowed my head and said, "I don't know."

I know why. But I didn't want to say. I knew that I would be in trouble, even though I was only four. My mother had issues, and I had already witnessed a lot of horrible things.

When Blane was finished, he looked at me. He said, "What are you boobing about?"

I had tears running down my face. I didn't even realize that I had been crying. It had been a long time since I had thought about that day.

FAMILY BOATING DAY

Even though Blane was not supposed to be around minors, he planned a boating day at the lake with his brother's widow and her young children. I told him it was not a good idea. He didn't listen to me. I knew he wouldn't. He never listened to me. I invited my children. Harmony didn't want to go. She hated Blane. Bennett came. His Dad and his wife also came. His Dad brought his boat.

I always kept a close eye on all the children, especially the little girl. She was about eight and beautiful. I didn't want anything to happen to them.

I was sitting in a lawn chair next to Bennett's stepmother, and she began telling me that Blane has never had any respect for authority, that he thinks he can do no wrong. That one of these days we were going to get caught and he would go back to prison. I was thinking how right she was. I was learning all this on my own.

All the kids had fun that day. Trying to learn how to ride the new board. It was a beautiful day. I was glad that Bennett had come. I really enjoyed the time with him. It seemed like whenever I was home, he would be off playing at a friend's.

FEELING TRAPPED

I told Blane I wanted to go home to spend some time with the kids. He said, "Why they don't care about you."

I said, "Yes they do."

hen I started to think maybe he is right. I called them to see what they were doing. They had plans, so I just stayed.

He wanted to have sex, and I said, "No I don't want to." That didn't matter. He picked me up and took me over to the bed. He stood me next to it and pulled my pants down to my ankle's. I turned my head to look at him and said, "Stop I don't want to do this."

He ignored me and bent me over the bed. I could hear him spit on his hand. He then took his hand and ran it between my legs to get it wet. Then placed his penis in me. He held my head into the mattress. I couldn't move or make a sound. It seemed like it went on forever.

I flashed back to what I had read in the report. This was exactly what the child said he did. Was he reliving that day? Did he imagine that I was her? I wanted to cry but didn't because he always got mad when I would. I did cry a lot but only when I was alone. I didn't want anyone to know what was happening to me. I was afraid they would think less of me.

When he was done, he calmly said, "Come on let's take a shower."

I followed him to the shower. He washed my hair and my body. He showed no sign of remorse. I told him I was going home.

He said, "If you go home, I'm going out. I'm not going to sit here alone. I will find someone to keep me company."

I knew that meant he was going to look for someone else. He knew that would upset me and it did. I ended up not leaving.

I had a hard time sleeping at his house. I always did from the start after that first night. I would also always be afraid that his Parole officer would show up in the middle of the night. I would hear all kinds of sounds coming from outside. I had to get a prescription from my Doctor because the stress was causing me to itch. Sometimes the itching would get so bad that I would scratch myself raw.

I stood that night looking out the window towards my house. I wanted to leave so bad. I knew that if I did, we would have a huge fight. I was torn. I wanted out but how. He always got me to come back. I would keep asking myself. "What is wrong with you? Why are you so weak?" I beat myself up all the time!

BACKHANDED

We decided to stop and pick up dinner for Bennett and us. When we arrived at my house, Bennett was riding his motorized scooter up and down the driveway. Blane said, "What are you doing riding that. Your grounded and have no privileges. You're just a little druggy."

We went into my room, and I called Bennett to come in so he could eat his food. Blane started talking more shit.

Bennett said, "Fuck you, Blane. Your nothing but a pedophile."

Blane back-handed Bennett. He lost his balance but didn't fall. He went running from the room. I said, "Blane what the hell is the matter with you as I went running out the door after Bennett."

Blane came out the door right behind me and said, "I'm leaving. I know I'm going back to prison for sure now."

At that moment, I didn't care what happened to him. I needed to get to my boy. He took off across the street to the church. I chased after him and finally caught him. I tried to hug him. He pushed me away and began screaming, "I'm calling my Dad. I'm going to tell him what he did."

I was immediately filled with fear. Bennett's Dad would take the kids from me. Again, I tried to hug him. He let me, and I held him and told him how sorry I was that happened. I told him if he told his Dad he would make him go live with him. Bennett hated his Dad, and that was that last thing he wanted. He didn't call him and tell him for fear of having to live with him.

I tried to call Blane. The first few times I called he didn't answer. He finally did and said, "I'm going to the mountains to meet God. Nobody can stop me. I'd rather die than go back to prison."

Then he hung up. I called repeatedly. He wouldn't answer. I called my girlfriend Sheryl and told her the situation. I asked her to call his phone and keep calling until he answered. Instead, she called his probation officer and told him that she believed he was in the mountains and was going to take his own life.

His parole officer called him, and he answered. A few minutes later he called me. He was pissed off and said, "What the fuck. Why would you call my probation officer?"

I said, "I didn't. It must have been Sheryl. I called her and told her that you threatened to kill yourself."

He said, "We'll I'm not. That was the stupidest thing she could have done. I need some time to think. I will talk to you later."

I stayed home that night. I wanted to be with Bennett. We watched a movie. He didn't say anything about what had happened earlier that day.

I went to Blane's the next day. He said, "If you call and report what happened you will go to jail too. They will take your kids, and you probably wouldn't be able to see them for a very long time. You will go to jail for failure to protect, your kids around me when you knew I had an order to not be around minors. Plus, you knew my charges. You also didn't call immediately and report it when I hit him. So, that makes you just as guilty."

Oh, my God, he was right. I was terrified. I didn't want to lose my kids. I didn't want to go to jail. What am I going to do.? I went home and told Bennett what he had told me.

Bennett said, "Don't worry mom I won't say anything. I love you and would never want to see you go to jail." Bennett held on to that secret.

I eventually told his parole officer.

FORCED FED

We would take turns cooking dinner. It was really hard for me. I'm a very picky eater. I hate vegetables. I always have.

One night Blane made dinner for the two of us. He decided to make spinach even though he knew I hated it. We were sitting at the dinner table when he told me to eat my spinach. I told him I was going to eat it. I don't like spinach.

He said, "You're going to eat that spinach."

I said, "No, I'm not."

Blane said, "You will eat it, or I will force you to eat it."

I said, "I'm not eating it."

He got up from his seat and came up behind me. He grabbed my head. Put spinach on my fork. He then forced my mouth open and shoved the spinach in my lips. He cut the corner of my mouth with the fork because I tried to keep my mouth closed so he couldn't put that slimy, nasty, spinach in my mouth. Once he had it in my mouth, he ordered me to swallow it. I did.

Blane said, "Now finish it. I just want you to be healthy. You need to eat more vegetables."

I just sat there. Finally, Blane said, "Fuck it. Just throw it away if you're not going to eat it."

I got up scrapped the remaining food in the trash then went and sat on the couch. I was fighting back the tears. I had learned not to cry and show no emotion.

He came and sat on the couch next to me. Picked up the remote and started scanning the channels.

I got up, and he said, "Where do you think you're going?"

said, "To do the dishes."

"Oh," he said.

I went over to do the dishes because I was having a hard time holding in tears. I was so angry. Not just at him but at me. Once again, I found myself beating myself up. What is wrong with you? Why do you take this? Do you hate yourself that much? I don't know how many times I have asked myself this.

Yet I stay.

BLACK OUT

Harmony and I had started drifting apart when I married Joe. Our relationship had become very distant due to my not being there. Both emotionally and physically, as a mother, I had dropped the ball.

One day I went down to her room, and we got into an argument. I can't even remember what it was about. We began to yell at each other. Harmony said something about her phone. I said something back. She assumed that I had taken it. She grabbed me by the throat and began choking me. I just stood there with my arms to my side and looked into her eyes. I saw nothing but hate and anger. She had every right to hate me. I had abandoned her. She continued to squeeze as hard as she could. My roommate's daughter Tatianna was trying to pull her hands off my throat as she was yelling for Harmony to let go. I began to see spots and felt as if I was going to black out. Just then she let go.

Tears began to roll down my face. I didn't say anything. I went out to my room and sobbed. I was crushed. I had no one to blame but myself.

A few months later we got into another argument. She came at me. This time I was going to defend myself. We ended up rolling around on the floor. I ripped out her new ear piercings. The next thing I remember is Bennett behind me pulling me off of Harmony.

He was screaming. "Mom stop!"

I was on top of Harmony hitting her in the face with my fists over and over. I froze. Oh, my God what have I done. I got up off of her and ran up the stairs. I jumped in my van and sped off. I couldn't stop crying.

In the sixteen years, I had Harmony I never hit her. I always knew that I could hurt them. That's why I didn't spank them. I have so much anger and hate inside of me that I'm afraid if I let it out I could hurt someone.

I stayed gone most of the day. When I got home, Harmony said, "Mom I need to talk to you."

"Okay," I said.

Harmony told me, "I don't feel good. I took a bunch of your pills."

She handed me the bottle. She had taken a bunch of Naproxen. I knew that she was not going to die from it. I called poison control, and they said she would be okay.

I knew that if I took her to the hospital, and told them what she had done, they would keep her. I told her we needed to go to the hospital. She needed help. In reality, we both needed help.

I took her to the hospital. They kept her just like I thought. I went to see her a couple of times. I wanted to go every visit. I didn't though because her Dad and grandparents were also going up to see her. I didn't want to have to interact with them.

I told the doctors that I was afraid of her, so they would give her the help she needed.

Harmony always thought that I was afraid of her. That I would back down from her because of my fear, when the truth was, I was afraid of me. What would happen if I let my anger out? I just found out that my fear was real. What I was afraid of happening happened.

Harmony and Bennett stayed at their grandparents for a while.

YUBA LAKE

Blane and I planned a boating trip in mid-August to take the family to Yuba Lake. We invited all of my family. My kids didn't want to go because he was going but changed their minds and decided to go anyway. The day before we were supposed to go, Blane said he didn't want to go.

At first, I was pissed. He was supposed to pull the boat, and I was going to tow the wave runners with my van. It was just another way for him to ruin things. He was always ruining any family time I had.

I went ahead and went. My nephew and great niece and their family came.

We didn't have the boat, but at least we had the wave runners. My nephews, camper got stuck in the sand. He tried to get it out with his truck. Then his truck got stuck. He called the Rangers, and they came to pull him out. Then they got stuck. They ended up having to get a backhoe to pull all the vehicle out. It was comical.

A couple of days before this weekend, Blane had come home from work. We were sitting on the couch, and he took his penis out. He grabbed my head and brought it down to his hard penis. I tried to pull back, but he forced it in my mouth. It tasted nasty. The first thing I thought was he had just been with someone. I could taste it. He moved my head up and down. He then took me over to the bed. He stood me next to it. He pulled my pants down. He took his leg and pressed it between my legs and then moved my legs apart. He then placed himself inside of me. I made no sound and no movement. I went somewhere else.

I started to have a discharge. The first day at Yuba my lower back started hurting. As the day went, on the pain got worse. I wasn't going to cancel this trip. I had been looking forward to it for too long just to leave. I sat in the van all that evening.

I would walk to the outhouse to use the restroom constantly. I felt like I had to pee and then nothing. Then the pain got so bad that I couldn't make the walk. I would step outside the van and go right there. I had a towel wrapped in a wad and placed it behind my back. The pressure would help to alleviate some of the pain but not all of it. I tried to keep drinking lots of water hoping that would help. The next day I felt a little better.

I sat on the beach and watched my family have fun on the wave runners. I was glad that Blane didn't come. There were too many kids.

Harmony and Bennett got stranded in the middle of the lake on one of the wave runners. Harmony told Bennett to get off. He began to drift away from her, and all you could see was his head. I was terrified that a boat was going to come along and decapitate him.

We were all yelling at him to swim back to her. My nephew Aden hurried over to them on the other wave runner. They managed to get the kids and the wave runner back to the beach. It was very frightening to watch my children in a bad situation and being unable to help them.

My niece's ex-husband, Aden had come up with his daughter, even though I hadn't invited him. When I told Blane that he was there he got mad. He accused me of planning that all along. He was jealous. I told him it wasn't my fault. Besides you're the one who bailed on me. He hung up. I tried to call back but no answer. I tried several times and finally thought oh we'll.

The day we were leaving everybody cleaned up the camp. We got the wave runners loaded on the trailer. Everyone left. Harmony, Bennett and I were driving toward the exit. We hit a bump and then there was a loud thump, and my van jerked. When they hooked the trailer back to my van, they had not secured it with the safety. So, it bounced off. I was still in a lot of pain but tried to lift it back on. All three of us tried and couldn't do it. I began to get very angry. I started to cry. A man pulled up behind us and lifted it back on. He said, "Be careful driving home and go slow."

I was upset that everyone had just taken off. I was upset because Blane wasn't answering his phone. I was mad because I was sure he was seeing that girl. I was angry.

When we got back to Salt Lake, I was in excruciating pain. I told Harmony that I needed to go to the hospital. I could barely stand up. I was burning up. Harmony took me to the hospital. She called Blane and told him that she was taking me. He showed up at the hospital, and I told Harmony she could leave if she wanted to. She decided to leave because she was tired. It had been a long weekend.

They began to run tests. They said I had a severe kidney infection and that it was a good thing that I came in. They gave me iv antibiotics and a prescription.

A week later it happened again, and this time it was even more painful. I went back to the hospital and once again they gave me antibiotics.

I called Blane and told him I was going back to the hospital. He showed up. Dressed up real nice. He usually didn't dress that way. I asked him why he was so dressed up. He had some bullshit story about having a meeting with some builders. I said, "Okay." I didn't believe him, but I was in no condition to argue. They gave me something stronger prescription this time.

I had a friend coming in that evening from California to race his car at Rocky Mountain Race Way. Even though I didn't feel right, we went to dinner with him and his whole racing team. We went to Totems for dinner. I introduced Denny to Blane. They started talking mechanics. Denny asked Blane if he would like to come to the track and work on his pit crew. Blane jumped at the chance. He loved working on cars, and he loved the races.

The next morning Blane decided that he needed to get his needs met. I was still hurting. He didn't care. He just did his usual, and I took it. I was so angry. I had to go clean a job that morning for him as well. He came to the job, and I wouldn't talk to him. He said, "What's your problem?"

I said, "I was in the hospital last night in major pain. All you ever think about is you. You didn't even care how painful that was for me this morning."

His usual response, "Whatever."

I told him I wasn't going to the races.

"Suit yourself," he said. He then left, and I remained at the job. It took me a better part of the day to complete it because I hurt so bad. I didn't go to the races that night.

The next morning, I was going to go out so I could see my friend. I called Blane and told him I was coming over. He said, "Hey just heads up. There is a girl here. She is Denny's friend, and she needed a place to stay last night."

I got to his house, and she was sitting at the table. He introduced us. She actually was Denny's friend. I was still upset and really didn't have much to say to her.

When we got to the track, Denny was in the semi, sitting on his bed. I sat next to him and told him why I hadn't come the day before. He said, "I'm sorry. That is totally messed up. I'm here for you if you need me."

I said, "Thank you." Then I gave him a hug. I stayed at the track the rest of the day. I gave Blane the cold shoulder for a while. Then, of course, he tried to make me the bad guy. Saying me and Denny had something going on. He was always good at taking the light of himself and shining it somewhere else when he was in the wrong.

MY BIRTHDAY AT THE LAKE

The week before my birthday he called me and told me to meet him at Ross department store at the Valley Fair mall. I asked why. He said, "It's a surprise." I got there before him and sat outside on the bench. It was a beautiful night. The sky was clear and a little breezy. He came walking up still in his work cloths. He had just got back in town. We went inside of the mall, holding hands. He led me to Morgan Jewelers. He stopped at the rings. He asked me what I liked. I told him you choose. We looked at several different styles. I wanted one that I could wear to work, so it had to be a band type without a diamond on top. We picked out a band made of white gold with several diamonds incrusted in it. It was beautiful. He put it on my finger and said, "I love you."

Sometimes he can do the sweetest things. He worked on my house, fixed my van and helped my family with stuff. If only he didn't have that dark side that takes control of his body. His need for sexual gratification is what makes him a monster.

September 15th, 2013 Blane, myself and the kids went boating at Pineview Lake. It was my birthday. The kids really didn't want to go, but they went because they knew it would make me happy. My kids loved me even though I had been a horrible mother.

It was a beautiful sunny day. The sky was blue, and there was a slight breeze. We were having an amazing day.

Bennett did not want to get in the water. Blane kept egging him on telling him to get in. Bennett continued to say no. Blane thought it would be fun to through him in. I told him don't do it. He didn't listen to me. He grabbed Bennett to toss him in. Bennett started kicking and swinging. He screamed at Blane to let him go. He didn't. Blane threw him into the lake. Bennett was screaming at him from the water. Saying how much he hated him. What a piece of shit he is. Blane just laughed.

I said, "What is the matter with you? He said he didn't want to get in the water. Thanks, you really fucked up a great day."

Blane's response, "Whatever."

Bennett remained angry most of the day. He wouldn't talk to anyone. He stayed wrapped in his towel. I sat next to him and apologized for Blane's actions. Bennett said he wished he hadn't come. I told him how glad I was that he did because I wanted to spend time with him. I haven't been able to spend much time with my kids. That's my fault. I don't know how to stand up for what I want.

dozed off on the ride home. I woke up when we pulled into my favorite donut shop. We asked if I could get a hot donut even though the hot light was not on. The lady said, "No." I told her it was my birthday. She still wouldn't do it.

Blane got rude with her and asked for her name. He said he was going to call the corporate office. He was going to let them know how rude she was. She was being rude. That's why Blane had gotten rude with her. We all got donuts and a drink.

I was really happy that my kids spent my birthday with me.

HIS MOTHER'S VISIT

I met Blane's mother at the beginning of summer when she and her husband stopped in town as they were heading to Washington. They stayed up at the lake. We took the boat up to see them. Blane's daughter, her husband, and their three children also came. That was the first time, Blane had met his grandkids. His daughter didn't have much to do with him. Her husband said to her, "Keep an eye on the girls." I don't think he meant for anyone to hear that but her. I thought to myself don't you worry. I will not take my eyes off of them.

We all played on the boat and rode the wave runners until late in the afternoon. It turned out to be a very nice day.

I was looking forward to seeing his mom again. I really liked her, and she was very kind to me.

I was cleaning Blane's apartment because his mom was going to be there the next day, for his birthday. As I was cleaning the apartment, his phone went off. He had accidentally left it on the kitchen table. I picked it up, and I read the text. It said,

"Hey, am I going to see you this weekend or are you going to be out of town."

I didn't recognize the name or the number, so I punched the number into my phone. It came up with Jill's name. I had saved her number from the other times she had called. He changed the name so I wouldn't know it was her. I immediately got sick to my stomach. I was anger. I reached into the refrigerator and grabbed a beer. It was only nine in the morning, but I needed something to calm me done.

Just a few minutes later my daughter Ali walked in the door. She took one look at me and said, "What's wrong?"

I began to tell her, but she said, "It's probably nothing mom. Don't let it bother you."

The Ali and Blane, so he could do some work at her office. I continued to clean and drink. I then took Blane's laundry to my house. I wanted to pour bleach all over them, but I didn't.

Later that afternoon when I was under his kitchen table washing the floor he asked me, "What's your problem?"

I said, "Nothing."

He said, "Bullshit. You have been a bitch all day."

I crawled from under the table and stood up. I said, "Really, I wonder why. Let me tell you why. Your little girlfriend texted you today. She wants to know if she can see you." I was a little drunk, and I'm sure I said a lot more.

Of course, he denied doing anything wrong. He began telling me that I needed to stop being so insecure, that it's pathetic. He did what he always does and turned it on me.

I had had enough. I was furious. I left and went home. He called my phone several times, and I didn't answer it.

The next day I was still very hurt and angry. I decided that I was going to go up the canyon to our special family spot. I took firewood and liquor. I was going to get plastered. I had asked Ali if she would pick me up later. I knew that I would be incapable of driving.

Later, I called Ali and told her I was ready to be picked up. I was wasted. It doesn't take much. She picked me up, and instead of taking me home she took me to his apartment.

His mother was already there. She came up and gave me a hug. As we hugged I whispered in her ear, "He's just like his father."

She said, "No he's not. He loves you. I know my son, and I know when he loves someone."

I thought to myself. You don't know him at all. You don't know the things he has done.

I went in their motor home where everyone was hanging out. I acted like everything was okay. They asked if I was hungry. I said, "No."

But they insisted that I eat something. Blane's parents had made stew. I said I didn't want any because I knew it was probably made with dear. They assured me, that is was not. His mom handed me a bowl of the stew. I ate a carrot. As soon as no one was looking, I scrapped it back in the pot. Blane started laughing, "See you liked it. It was elk."

I said, "Really I didn't eat it."

I sat on his lap and was all lovey. I had a plan brewing.

We went up to bed. He turned away from me. I told him I was cold and he ignored me. He was suddenly giving me the cold shoulder.

I got up and went downstairs. His son was staying the night. He had built a fire in the pit, and he was drinking Yager. I decided to drink with him. We talked and drank for quite a while. I went to stand up to go to bed, and I couldn't get up.

A few minutes later Blane came down stairs.

He said, "You need to come upstairs and go to bed."

I told him, "I can't stand up. I have already tried."

He picked me up and carried me upstairs. He took me into the bathroom. He took my clothes off of me. He turned on the shower and pushed me in. It was freezing. He turned and walked away. I hurried to adjust the temperature. After I had got the water warm, I sat down on the shower floor and cried.

I got out and dried off. I made my way over to the bed. I got in, laid on my side with my back facing him. I was glad that he left me alone. He left the next morning without saying a word to me.

I didn't care. I was still upset.

I had called Jill a couple of times that day before I went to the canyon to drink. I hung up each time. I didn't know what to say. Finally, I talked to her. She was shocked. We talked for a bit and made plans to meet the next day.

MEETING JILL

Blane left the next morning without saying goodbye. I didn't give a shit. I had a big day planned. I was going to meet Jill.

We arranged to meet in the parking garage of the Grand America. I wanted to book a room there for Blane's special birthday surprise. I got lost in there and became very disorientated and upset. Someone from security told me I not to be so loud and asked me to leave. I told him, I would if I could find my way out. He led me to the elevator that led to the parking garage. I could feel them watching me the whole time I was there. I was not dressed for a such a high-class place. I had on my work sweats and a tee shirt. I had told Blane's mother that I had to go to work.

When I got back down to the parking garage, I saw Jill's car. I walked over to it. I told her I would be right back. I had to get Tiffany out of my car. I got in her car; Tiffany went crazy. She jumped in her lap; her whole body began squirming as she licked her face. She obviously knew Jill. Jill was hugging her.

She said, "I've missed you, Tiffany." He had obviously been taking my dog to her house.

We talked about Blane. We talked about the times he would see her. We compared all the lies he had told us. I was not angry with her. It was Blane who was in the wrong. I asked her if she could help me with something. She said, "Yes." I told her I would need her to be free next Saturday night. She said she would make sure she was available.

I went over to Little America and booked a room for the next Saturday. I was putting together a Birthday he would never forget.

I stopped at the store on my way back to Blane's place. I found the perfect birthday card. When you open it, it plays my wish for you by Rascal Flatts. I thought to myself, how perfect.

I wrote. Blane, I love you so much. I'm so sorry that I am so insecure. It's because I love you more than anything in the world. I just want you to be happy. That is my wish for you. That everything you want comes true. I will do whatever I have to, to make all your dreams come true. Just know you are my world. I have planned a special birthday for just the two of us next weekend.

Loving you always.

BLANES BIRTHDAY DINNER

I went back to the shop after I made the reservations for the birthday present I was giving Blane the following Saturday.

He was in his mom's motorhome having a glass of wine. I walked in; his mom asked me if I'd like some wine. I said, "No, Thank you. I drank more than enough last night."

Blane and I went inside his apartment. He acted like everything was great between us. It was always like that. He would just go on with life as if there were no problems.

We all met at the restaurant that evening. Blane's mom, stepDad, Dad, stepmother, my parents, his son, his daughter, her husband and his mom. Yes, it was the ex-girlfriend again.

Blane was opening his cards and gifts. After he opened my card and read it, he gave me a big kiss and said, "I love you."

I replied, "I love you too." All the while, thinking to myself. You stupid asshole. Just wait for that birthday surprise. I was so excited about what I had planned for him. It's what was keeping me from falling apart.

Blane handed my card across the table to his mom. She began reading it. She then started to cry. I felt bad because I really liked his mom.

I managed to keep my emotions under control for the rest of his mother's visit. I didn't want to ruin her vacation, with our problems. The next morning, she left; I fell to the floor sobbing because I knew she would hate me after I finished what I had to do.

All that week I had to act like everything was good between us. I cringed every time he touched me. I was so angry and hurt. I didn't let him know that. I would cry every time I left his house.

My kids could hear me crying in my room. I cried for a week straight.

THE BIG SURPRISE

It was Saturday. The sky was blue, and I could tell that fall was here. I had been busy all week putting my birthday surprise together for Blane. I told him I had to do a cleaning that morning. I lied.

I picked up my girlfriend, Jenny. We met up with Jill at the Little America hotel. We went up to the room that I had reserved the week before. We needed to know the layout. We sat up the alarm clock camera that I had purchased online. I had to have my son show me how to use it. I obviously didn't learn what I needed to because it didn't film anything. I was really bummed out about that. I would have loved to be able to watch that evening over and over. After we had discussed things, I took Jenny back to my house. My roommate was going to give her a ride to the hotel when it was time.

I went back to Blane's apartment. He had been working on a car all day. We were upstairs in his apartment; I told him I was going to go home and get ready.

I said, "I will come pick you up. Blane, I will never ask you this again, but I need to ask this last time. Have you been with anyone else since we have been together?"

He looked me dead in the eye and said, "I haven't put my dick in anyone else's hole."

I said, "Okay, I won't ask you that again. I love you. I will be back to get you in just a bit."

As I drove home, I couldn't quit crying. He will never admit it. I gave him the chance to come clean. If he had, I would have stopped what was about to happen. I had to carry through with my plan.

I picked him up. I was dressed to kill. I had a black dress on, high heels and I had put on makeup. He was dressed in a nice dress shirt and had on his cowboy boots. He looked nice.

I suggested we stop by my house. Everyone there knew what was going to happen that night. I had Harmony take some pictures of us. I was holding Tiffany. Blane was so happy. He had been looking forward to tonight ever since I gave him the card. I even had him look at something on Harmony's car. I took a picture of him next to her. Proof he had been in the presence of a minor.

We went to the Steak Restaurant in Little America. They had just remodeled, the place we had our first lunch was no more. We sat across from each other. The table cloth was white; there were candles on the table.

His son called him. Blane told him how nice the place was. He had the biggest smile. I was filming him while he was talking with his boy.

He said, "He'd like to get a bottle of wine." It was eighty dollars. He said, "I will split the cost of it with you."

I said, "No let me buy it for you, honey. This is your special night." I bought him that bottle of wine.

I excused myself from the table to go to the restroom. Jenny and Jill were in the restroom waiting for me. I told them to go up in fifteen minutes. Make sure you stay out of sight.

We left the restaurant and got on the elevator to go to our room. My heart was pounding. I was so excited. I couldn't wait to see the look on his face. We got off the elevator. When we entered the room, he said, "I'm going to go get some ice."

I said, "No, let me go get it."

He said, "I'll go get it."

My heart started pounding. I was afraid he was going to see them. I turned on the radio. I made sure it was romantic music. I ran him a bath while I waited for him to return.

He came back in with the ice. He didn't mention anything. I was relieved. I took him into the bathroom and undressed him. He got into the bath tub. I began washing him. He stood up and got out of the tub. I dried him off and then went down on my knees. I placed his cock into my mouth and began to move back and forth. I then stood up and kissed him passionately. I took the towel and wrapped it around him. On the bathroom counter, next to the pink bag, which had a piece of lingerie sticking out the top, was the tie for the robe. I picked it up to place around his eyes.

He said, "What are you doing?"

I said, "Honey, please let me put this on you. I have a very special evening planned. Don't ruin it."

He let me put it on him. I led him over to the bed. I had him lay in the middle. I kissed him again. I told him I would be right back. I was going to change. I went into the bathroom and took his clothes, wallet, phone, keys and boots and stuffed them in a bag I had hiding in the closet. I quietly crept over to the door and opened it. I handed Jenny the bag. Jill slipped in. We quietly walked over to the bed. She was on one side and me on the other. We took our index finger and ran it up his leg. We both sat on the edge of the bed. We looked at each and smiled. At the same time, we turned on the lamps.

Blane said, "What the fuck is going on?" as he pulled off the blindfold.

I said, "Tell me you haven't been fucking her for the past nine months."

He looked at me and said, "Yeah so." Then he jumped up and started yelling. We panicked and took off out the door. I got down to the lobby and called him on the house phone. He told me he had called security and I better bring his stuff back.

I looked over towards the lobby. There were guys in suits with radios; they were looking for someone. I ran out to get his stuff. My friends were driving away with it. I had to stop them. I got his stuff and hurried back to the room. When I entered the room, the phone rang. It was security. He told them that he got his stuff back. Just then there was a loud knock on the door. They yelled this is security.

I looked at Blane and said, "You better say this was a prank. I will make your life a living hell if you don't."

We walked over to the door and opened it. There were several security guards standing in the hall. Blane had his arm over my shoulder, and I had my arm around his waist. I told the security officers that he was always playing pranks on me and that I had done this as a prank and didn't think it all the way through. I told them I was really sorry. He is really mad at me.

The security guard said, "As he should be." They were happy with that and left.

Once they were gone, I began crying. I was yelling at him. How could you do this to me? I fell to my knees and placed my head in my hands and began sobbing. He put his hand on my head. He then said, "I'm leaving I not going to put up with this bullshit." He took a taxi home.

After he had left I went out to the balcony. It was still light enough to see the city. As I was standing there, I began thinking. What's the use? Why do I even go on anymore? I looked down; I was up high enough.

I then thought about my grandmother. When I was twelve, the phone rang. I answered it. It was my grandma, Rita. I yelled for mom that grandma was on the phone.

I said, "I love you, grandma."

Before she could say anything back, my mother snatched the phone out of my hand. My mom started yelling at her and then slammed the phone down. It didn't really phase me because they were always fighting.

A short time later we were walking out the front door to go to church. As we were walking to the car, a police car pulled up in front of the house. My mom walked over to them.

They were talking to my mom; she began crying, she covered her face with her hands. She was sobbing uncontrollably. She walked towards us and told us to go back into the house. Once we got into the house, she told us to sit on the couch.

She said, "Grandma killed herself. She jumped off a building."

I cried so hard; I loved my grandma. I'm so glad that I was able to tell her that I loved her.

Then I heard a knock at the door. It startled me at first. I went and opened the door. It was Jenny. She saw my tear-streaked face, she hugged me and said, "Everything is going to be okay?"

I then started laughing. I said, "You should have seen the look on his face. It was priceless."

I said, "I spent a lot of money on this room were not going to let it go to waste."

We went downstairs to the bar. We started drinking. It didn't take long for me get wasted. I'm such a lightweight; a few drinks is all it takes.

We went back to the room. I messaged a friend on Facebook. A few minutes later I get a text from Blane. He had my Facebook password and saw that I had messaged an old friend. He immediately started accusing me of being the cheater. WOW, I just ignored him.

I wasn't going to let him try to make me think that I was doing something wrong. Once, again he wanted to make me the bad guy. He certainly wasn't going to take any responsibility for his actions.

CHANCE MEETING

The next day I had made plans to go to dinner with Joe. We went to our favorite restaurant the Long Horn. We went there for all our special occasions. We also went when there wasn't anything special.

As we were walking to our table, I heard my name. I looked over and saw my nephew and his friend sitting at the table. They waved us over. They asked if we'd like to join them.

I said, "Sure that would be great."

Joe and I sat down with them and ordered drinks. We sat with them the whole time.

I went to the bathroom; my nephew's date came in. She asked how I was doing? I told her what I had just done to Blane. She thought it was great and that he deserved it.

I ended up staying the night at Joe's. Blane kept calling. I just ignored the calls. I had nothing to say. I finally just turned it off because he would not give up.

A few months back, he had given me an
ultimatum; him or Joe. I had to quit talking to him or
seeing him. Of course, I told him I choose you. I
never gave up on Joe. Joe meant too much to me. I
was not going to let someone force me to do that. I
talked to Joe every day on the phone. When I was in
his neighborhood or when I had time, I would see
him. If I didn't have time, I would do what I had to, to
make the time.

ATTEMPTED SUICIDE

I finally answered the phone the next day. He
asked me where I had been. I said, "It's none of your
business. I don't have to tell you anything. Just leave
me alone." Then I hung up.

He called back. I answered he said, "If I you leave me I have nothing to live for." Then he hung up. I tried to call back, but he wouldn't answer.

I called his mother. As soon as she heard my voice, she said, "Leave my son alone. You, stupid bitch." Then she hung up. I was calling her to tell her that I thought Blane was going to kill himself.

I went to his apartment. I was frantic. I couldn't live with myself if he did something like that. I would feel responsible.

I got there, and he was watching TV. Once, again I was duped, I was pissed, and he knew it.

I told him I'm going home. I'm not playing your games.

When I got home, I went down to Harmony's room. I knocked on the door. She didn't answer so I hit it harder. I then turned the door knob. It was unlocked, as I opened the door, she stood up. She was completely naked.

Bennett walked up behind me, and as soon as he saw her naked, he ran back to his room. I asked her who was in there with her.

She said. "No one." I kicked the blankets on the floor really hard and up popped a boy.

She began screaming at me, "I hate you! Why don't you just go kill yourself? Nobody wants you. Nobody loves you. Blane doesn't even love you. That's why he cheated on you. You're a piece of shit. You are a horrible mother. Do everybody a favor mom and go kill yourself."

I knew at that moment that she was right. I was a horrible mother. I was a horrible person. Everyone would be better off. I had hurt so many people. I was no good for anyone.

I went out to my room in tears. I knew what I needed to do. Bennett had followed me out there. I opened my safe. I grabbed my bottle of hydrocodone and Xanax.

Bennett asked me what I was doing. I told him I was going to stay at a friend's house. I gave him a hug. I was sobbing. "Bennett, I love you so much. You are a good boy," I said.

I knew what I was about to do and it was breaking my heart. I felt like I had no other options. I was hopeless. I couldn't break away from this man. I couldn't stop him from doing the things he was doing to me. I had made a mess out of my life and my kid's lives. I got in my car and headed to the family spot in the canyons.

On my way, there I called Blane crying hysterically. I told him "I couldn't handle life anymore. I didn't want to live. That I was going to end it all."

He said, "I'm not dealing with your bullshit Julee. I'm going to bed, and he hung up.

I then called my ex-husband and said, "You win." Then I hung up.

Why did I tell him you win? In our marriage, he had told me to kill myself several times, that the world would be a better place without me in it. I was just letting him know his wish was coming true.

I stopped at the 7-eleven at the mouth of the canyon. I wiped my face and calmed down before I went in. I bought a beer to drink with the pills. Hoping that would make them start working faster. It was late about eleven. I knew there wouldn't be anybody up there because the day sites were closed for the season.

I pulled into the parking lot. I left my van unlocked with the keys and my wallet sitting on the seat. I didn't want them to have to break the window to get inside.

I'm not afraid of dying. Back in 1985, I died. It was amazing. I was moving towards an illuminating white energy that moved back and forth, next to it stood Brett. The feelings I felt are so hard to describe. It was total peace and pure joy. I haven't felt those feeling since that day. Just as Brett and I were reaching our arms out towards each other, my eyes suddenly flew open.

There was a bright light above my head; standing all around the bed where doctors and nurses. One of the doctors said, "You're lucky to be alive." He was holding the heart paddles in his hands.

What I'm lucky to be alive? I didn't feel lucky at all.

Later I started to believe that God had a plan for me. He wasn't ready for me to come home. I believe that those who experience the afterlife have the experience God feels they need them to have. I know without a doubt that I was in heaven. I believe he showed me my purpose. I had a baby girl who needed a mommy. I feel that he just wanted me to know that Brett was okay.

I have so much more I need to share about my life with Brett; about his murder. That is a book all of its own.

I walked over to our picnic table. It was so quiet and peaceful. I immediately opened the beer and the pill bottles. I took them all. I didn't want to live anymore. I figured if the pills didn't kill me the cold would. As I began to feel the effects of the pills, I saw something. It was lights, at the top of the trail. Then I heard voices. I stood up and threw the pill bottles out into the river. I climbed under the picnic bench hoping that they wouldn't see me. Then everything went black.

The next thing I remember is my face being cradled in the hands of an angel. She had beautiful green eyes full of compassion. She said, "Julee it's going to be all right. We love you and were here for you. God loves you, and he will never leave you. Everything is going to be all right." She was definitely one of my guardian angels. She had turned out to be one of my best friends and just like she said she is and had been there for me.

I guess my ex-husband had tried to call me back on my phone. The kids answered it and told him the situation. He went to the hospital, but he didn't notify any of my family. I was out for two days. They were concerned that I might have suffered some brain damage, so they ran some tests while I was still unconscious. He was probably hoping I would wake up and have no one there so that I could feel like no one cared.

I woke up in a dark room, all alone.

I just laid there. I didn't know where I was. I sat up, and my head began spinning. Then I remembered that I had taken a bunch of pills. They must have found me. I finally got up and walked slowly to the door. I felt like I was going to fall.

My chest hurt so bad. It felt like an elephant had been sitting on it. I found out later they had given me Narcon. I'm sure they also had to do CPR. I opened the door and stepped out. I stayed up against the wall and made my way down to a little window. It was the nurse's station. I had been taken to LDS psychiatric ward.

I was so upset. I wanted to be dead. This isn't fair. I don't want to be here anymore. Once again God had intervened. He must have some plan for my life. But what I'm so tired of the way my life has been thus far.

The nurse at the station turned to one of the aides and told her to move me to the room next to the station. They had it set up, so they were able to see in the room.

Later that day, a doctor came to talk to me. I knew I had to get out of there. I had to say what they wanted to hear. I know how this all works.

So, I did just that. I told him that I wasn't trying to kill myself. I was just upset. I didn't realize I had taken so much. I told him that keeping me in there would just compound my problems. I needed to get out because my boy had court. His Dad would get him, and that would not be in my son's best interest.

I was out the next day. No seventy-two-hour hold. I know how to act when I need to make something happen. I had learned what it takes to survive.

Blane came to see me while I was in the hospital. He brought me some panties, socks and pink slippers with sequins all over them. I said, "If I put those on and tap my feet together will I get to go home." He laughed.

The panties he brought were granny panties. I held them up and said, "Really."

He said, "I just grabbed what I saw. I told him, thank you. He said, "I have to go to Richmond and finish the job. Dad said it has to be done asap. You will need to find a ride home. I think that you should go stay at my place so that you can rest."

"Okay," I said.

Then he started asking me all kinds of questions. He asked, "Why was Kerk at the hospital? Were you guys hanging out together?"

I said, "I called him on my way up the canyon. To tell him he had won because he had told me many times to just kill myself. I don't know how he ended up there."

I didn't know. I didn't know anything at that point.

SIDE EFFECTS

I had really screwed myself up. I had diarrhea for several weeks after. Every time I would eat something it would go straight through me. I wouldn't eat because I was afraid I wouldn't make it to the bathroom on time. I had to borrow my Dad's potty chair and put it in my room. I couldn't remember a lot of stuff.

My first day back to work I walked into the bathroom and just stood there. Where do I start? How did I use to clean this?

I walked into the kitchen with tears in my eyes. Sheryl said, "What's wrong?"

After I had explained she said, "It is okay Julee everything will become clearer. It's just going to take some time." She then walked back to the bathroom with me and said, "You always started with the shower, then the toilet and then mirror, sink, cupboards then the floor."

I just felt so overwhelmed and confused.

I stayed away from my family for a while. I didn't want them to know what I was dealing with. I would stutter sometimes, and words would come out all scrambled. My friend Stewie thought it was funny and said, "I'm going to start putting these words in my phone."

I didn't remember a lot of things. I couldn't focus on anything. I was so afraid that I had really damaged myself this time. I didn't realize the extent of my memory loss until the memories came flooding back.

DETAINED

It was November 4, 2013, a Tuesday. Blane saw his parole officer on the first Tuesday of the month. I would always be on pins and needles on that day. Wondering if this was going to be the day they would arrest him.

This was the day. I waited for his call. He would always call me as soon as he left. Today I didn't get the call. Late that afternoon I got a call from the county jail. He was detained for dating me.

He said, "I need you to come see me tonight."

I said, "Okay."

I went to the jail that night to see him. He was giving me directions on what I need to do with his paperwork and bank stuff. He told me I need to go to property in the morning to get his keys, phone, and wallet. He said, "You need to fill out a visit form for the prison because I'm going back." He started crying. Begging me not to leave him. Telling me, he needed me.

How can I just abandon him? He needs me.
He is back here partly because of me. I had so many
emotions going on all at once.

I was still not doing very well. It had only
been a couple of weeks since I had ingested all of
those pills.

I had a spare key to his van. His Dad asked me
to bring it to his house. I did. I started taking stuff out
of it and putting it in my van. His Dad stopped me.
He told me to leave the stuff; he would take care of it.
Blane had told me to take his stuff because the last
time he was in prison, he lost everything. His Dad
was supposed to take care of it, and he didn't. I
grabbed the briefcase that had his brand-new
computer in it, and he asked me if it was mine. I said,
"Yes, it's mine." It wasn't, but I certainly wasn't
going to leave it with him.

A few days later I had to go to Blane's place to get Harmony's car that we had parked over there. His brother Dale was there. I was alone. He began screaming at me. Blaming me for Blane going back to prison. He said he was going to kill me and my whole fucking family. I will go to prison and not even care. You need to get off this property now.

I called his Dad and told him what was going on. He told me to get in my car. He would be right over. He called Dale, I don't know what he said, but he changed his behavior instantly.

Harmony's car had a flat tire. He got a pump out and began filling it. He didn't say anything to me. He just did it. I drove the car off the property and parked it. His Dad got there as I was walking back in the yard. He said, "Just ignore Dale. He is just angry."

"I'm so sorry Dad," I told him.

He said, "You both knew you were playing with fire. That this was inevitable, it was only a matter of time."

"Yeah, I know," I said.

I got in my van and left. I returned a short time later and retrieved the car from where I had parked it.

LETTERS

I received a letter about a week after he had been arrested. They moved him to the prison the day after they detained him. He told me he loved me. Blane asked me to get our friends and family members to write letters to the parole board telling them how he had helped them; to say good things about him. He was hoping that if he showed them, he had been doing positive things while he was out that they would go easy on him. He was terrified because they could have made him complete his sentence which would have been more 12 years.

In late December, they had a parole hearing at the Utah state prison. His Dad had notified me of the date and time.

At the time, I had mixed emotions about what I wanted to happen. I still loved him even though he had hurt me in ways that no one should be hurt. He isolated me from everyone. He had done so many things to me that I should have wished for him to get the maximum punishment. I hated myself for wanting him to not get the worst punishment.

I went to his parole hearing. His Dad and youngest daughter were also there. I sat next to them. When they took us into the room, he was already in there. His back was facing us. The judge came in, and everyone stood up. Blane was in shackles. Tears began rolling down my cheeks. The judge started talking and said what he had done. He also stated some other things he had done while out on parole. Blane didn't agree with one of the allegations. He tried to explain what happened. The judge acted like he didn't want to hear it but listened anyway. The judge ordered him to do a year for the violation. The judge said that he could turn around and say goodbye to us. He turned around and said, "I'm sorry. I love you guys." The guard then walked over to him and took hold of his arm and led him away.

I stood in the parking lot with his Dad and daughter for a few minutes. I couldn't quit crying. His daughter said I'm sorry Julee. We gave each other a hug and then we all went our separate ways.

VACATION WITH THE KIDS

It was Thanksgiving week, and I decided that the kids and I were going to go on vacation. Blane was back in Prison and couldn't stop me from doing it. We went to Las Vegas where my two best friends each from a different period of my life lived. We then went down to Los Angeles and saw some of my other friends. We went to the beach, universal studios and Big Bear.

Big Bear is where my mom lived before she passed. My brothers still lived there, so we paid them a visit. It was so nice to spend this time with the kids. I had missed so much. We all enjoyed ourselves. This is the last vacation that Bennett went on. He has been locked up, or on the run for all the other trips, we have taken. A lot of the trip I can't remember because my mind was still so foggy from all of the pills I had taken to end my life.

When we got home we were all so tired we went in and went right to bed. Big mistake.

Someone broke into the van and took our camera and a lot of other stuff. We were all so upset. They took all of our memories that were stored in that camera. Harmony was really upset because they stole all of her shoes. She took almost every pair she owned.

She loves shoes.

VISITATION

I was receiving letters from Blane about every other day. They moved him from the state prison a few weeks after his parole hearing. The day after they moved him I got a letter from the prison approving my visits. That did me no good. He wasn't their anymore. They moved him down to Fillmore county jail. He called me as soon as he got there. He told me I could come and visit; all I needed was my driver's license.

I drove down the next Sunday. It was a two-and-a-half-hour drive. They let you visit for three hours because of the distance you had to come to visit. It was really hard sitting there for that amount of time. The seats were hard, the room was small, and you had to hold the phone to your ear. After a while, my ears would start hurting from holding the phone against them.

He was so glad to see me. Tears began to roll down his face when he was telling me how much he missed me. How much he loved me. How he can't wait for us to get past this and start our future. How it would be so different. That he was so sorry for hurting me. How we would make sure we do it right this time. He wanted to marry me. How he wouldn't hurt me anymore. He asked me to forgive him for being with Jill.

He said, "The only reason I was with her was because I love you so much I was afraid that you wouldn't stay with me. I couldn't bear to be alone if you left me. You were too good to be true, so I was waiting for the inevitable; your leaving me. So, I had someone to fall back on."

We would put our hands up on the glass. It was so hard for me every time I went to see him. The drive took its toll on me. I began having my roommate Coby drive me down. It made the long trip so much easier having the company and not having to drive.

Blane had made friends with the pastor of a small church that was in Fillmore. I started going to church down there when I would go see Blane, which was almost every Sunday. The pastor and his wife were very kind and loving people. They would do services in the jail every week. They let me know how he was doing.

VINDICTIVE VALENTINES

Valentine's day was approaching. I couldn't help but remember last years. How my feelings had been hurt. So, I decided that I would let him see how it feels to be hurt. I called my friend Trek and asked him if he would like to go to the club.

Trek was a guy both Blane, and I knew from auto zone. We bought a lot of our parts from him for the cars we were fixing up. Trek was always joking and teasing me. We had become good friends.

Coby, Trek and I went to the club that night. I knew Blane would be calling me. When he did, he could hear the music in the background. He asked me where I was. I told him. He asked who I was with.

I said, "Cody and Trek." He didn't say anything for a minute.

He said, "You're there with Trek. What is he your date?"

I said, "Whatever."

I could hear the hurt and disappointment in his voice. I didn't feel bad at all. I thought to myself. So how does it feel? I was still holding onto a lot of hate, anger, and hurt.

STEWIE

Sheryl had been working for me for several years off and on and was working with me during this time. She was my best friend. She had a heart of gold and would help anyone she could. She was always letting people stay at her house when they were down on their luck.

Stewie was one of those people. I knew him from when I would go to CA meetings in my past. He was renting a room from her. Stewie looked so much like my ex-husband. He acted like him in a lot of ways to. He was always making passes at me. I explained that I was not interested. I was waiting for Blane. I also couldn't get past the resemblance he had to my ex. Big turn off.

I always picked Sheryl up for work. I made a point of going over early so we could have coffee. We would talk about what was going on in our lives. Sometimes we would gossip. Okay, a lot of times. One morning as I was sitting at the table there was a pill container on it with Stewie's name on it. There were a lot of pills in it. I said, "Damn Stewie you take a lot of pills."

He said, "There just vitamins."

I didn't think anything of it and sat the container back down.

We started hanging out. I paid him to do some work at my house that Blane had started. It was left unfinished when he went to jail. He was involved in drug court, and I wanted to help him. Giving him those side jobs helped him pay for it.

He would laugh and tease me when I was having a hard time talking. He joked when weird words would come out of my mouth. I really started to care about him.

He came by the house on Easter Sunday. I had just had a family get together. My daughter Ali was still there. She had been drinking and was a little drunk. She got anger when he went over and opened my trailer like he belonged there. She started yelling at him, and he said a few things back. He was holding his phone in his hand recording her. We got out to the front yard.

Ali said, "My mom is waiting for my Daddy. All you want is her putananie."

I just looked at her, trying my hardest not to start laughing.

Stewie said, "I'm your mom's friend. That's all we are."

He just shook his head and went and got in his car. He called me after he left. He said, "That was crazy."

I said, "I know. She loves Blane. She just wants me to be with him when he comes home."

Stewie graduated from drug court on August 30th. I was so proud of him. He had held down the same job.

He had tried to kiss me a couple of times. Every time he did, I would turn my head. Then I would tell him that I was not going to be unfaithful.

We had planned a trip to Wendover to celebrate his graduation. The morning we were supposed to go he called me. It was eight in the morning. He was very upset. He said, "Please come help me. I used, and I'm too high."

I got in my car and hurried over. His drug of choice was heroin. I kept visualizing him lying on the floor when I got there. I was frantic. I got there and went into his room. He was sitting on the edge of the bed with his head in his hands. I called his name. He looked at me, and I looked at him. Then he said, "Don't look at me."

He was embarrassed and ashamed.

I said, "Come on get your bag together. We have a room booked in Wendover."

We had to go to my house to get my things because I hurried over there when he called. I asked him if he had any more drugs and he said, "No."

I believed him. He had never lied to me before, so I had no reason to not trust him. We were close to the last store before Wendover when he asked if I would stop. He said that he needed some water.

I said, "Sure." I assumed he was thirsty, but that was not the case.

We got back on the freeway, and he started to get stuff out of his bag. I asked him what he was doing. He said, "I just need to do a little."

I said, "What the fuck!! You said you didn't have anything else." I looked in the rearview mirror there was a highway patrol behind us. I told him to stop. Put that shit away. There's a cop behind us. They stayed with us for a long time. We were close to Wendover at this point, so he decided to wait.

We pulled in the parking lot at the casino. He said, "Wait just a minute." He got his stuff out. He said, "Keep an eye out for me."

I was furious. I started yelling at him.

He said, "Stop you're going to draw attention to us."

I said, "I don't care. You said you didn't have any more of that shit."

He said, "Just watch for me PLEASE."

I kept an eye out for him.

We went to the hotel desk, and they said our room wasn't ready. We were there too early. I asked them if we could use the pool while we waited.

They gave us a pool key. I went in to change. I came out, and he was still not done changing. He was in the restroom for a long time. I started to get worried. Then he came walking out. He sat in a chair the whole time we were out at the pool. I swam most of the time we were out there. When I did sit at the table, I didn't speak to him. I was still very angry.

After finished swimming, we went to the casino to the gift shop and bought a six pack of beer. We sat over by the place you make bets on the races. I started drinking a beer. It takes me a long time to drink. He said, "Are you going to nurse that all day."

said, "Whatever." I chugged it and then another and another. Before knew it, I was drunk. I forgot that the beer in Nevada has a higher alcohol content.

I stumbled back up to the hotel desk to see if we could get our room. They said it was ready. He had to help me to our room. When we got in there, he laid me on the bed. He went into the bathroom. A few minutes later he yelled at me. "Julee come here." I got up and stumbled into the bathroom.

He said, "Let me see your arm." I stretched my arm out to him. I saw that he had a spoon on the counter. He had a syringe in his hand. He was moving it towards my arm. I didn't stop him. I just watched as he put it in my arm. He pulled back the plunger. Then I saw my blood enter into it. Then he pushed the drugs into my vein. It wasn't heroin. It was speed.

I walked back over to the bed. I just sat there. What the fuck did I just do? I hadn't put a needle in my arm since January 2003. I then began going through my purse; cleaning it out.

We did several more shots throughout the night. The last shot we did, he told me to do it myself. I was having a hard time doing it. He said, "You're going to have to learn to do that yourself. I'm not going to do it for you all the time."

I froze. I thought to myself, do this. I'm not going to do this after I leave here. He thought he had a sucker on the line. Someone who was going to support his habit. I don't think so. I'm done. I went into the bathroom. I looked in the mirror. I started to talk to God.

said, "God what have I done. Please forgive me". Then I started telling myself what a dumb ass I was. You're an idiot. Now you have really thrown your life away." I walked back into the other room. Stewie asked me who I was talking to. I played stupid and said, "What? You must be hearing things."

I laid down and finally dozed off. When I woke up, he wanted to go back to Salt Lake. I could tell he wanted more dope. Not me. I just wanted to go home. I wanted to end this nightmare.

On the ride, home I looked at him and asked, "Are you clean. Do I have anything to worry about."

He said, "No you don't have a thing to worry about."

I said, "Good. I already had to go through treatment for a year for Hepatitis C. I would hate to have to go through another treatment for anything."

Sheryl called me the next morning. She said, "I think Stewie is using."

I said, "Are you sure"?

Sheryl said, "Not totally but he is acting strange."

I said, "I don't think he is. He seemed fine the last time I saw him."

I lied to her because I didn't want her to know what I had done.

A few days later we were driving to one of our cleaning jobs. I couldn't stand the fact that I had lied to her. So, I told her what had happened in Wendover.

She said, "Did Stewie tell you he was HIV positive?"

I said, "What!! Are you kidding me?"

Sheryl said, "NO. He said he was going to tell you. He didn't tell you?"

I said, "No he didn't."

I immediately called and canceled my job. I drove straight to the health department. I went in and got tested. I told them the whole story. I gave them his full name so they could look him up in the data base.

Sheryl told Stewie that she wanted him out of her house. She didn't say anything about me knowing he had HIV. She called and told me he was coming to get his stuff. I told her I would be right over. Don't tell him I'm coming. I had arrived at her house before he did so I parked my van down the street. I waited for him in his room. When he walked in, I slammed the door shut behind him and locked it. I shoved him, picked up his pill container and said, "What the fuck are these Stewie?"

I then threw the container against the wall. His pills flew everywhere. I then swung my fist at him he caught my arm, twisted me around and slammed me into the door. He had me pinned. He was calling me a crazy bitch. He then said he was calling the police. He was going to have me charged with assault.

I said, "That's just fine with me. Call them." I went out onto the porch where Sheryl and Stewie's girlfriend were sitting. I said, "He is going to call the cops."

Sheryl said, "You should leave. They might take you to jail."

I said, "I'm not leaving. Let them take me to jail. They need to know what he did."

I waited for them to arrive. While I was waiting, I kept telling him what a loser he was. How he just threw the awesome opportunity, he had to have a relationship with his kids away. How he didn't care about anything but himself. I sat there and told his girlfriend what I mistake she was making by getting back with him. They hadn't been together in months because she was still using. I guess they were made for each other; they were both going nowhere.

The police took forever to get there. I walked over the officer's car. I told him the whole story. It made him angry. I could tell his whole demeanor changed. The officer said he wouldn't have been standing if he had done that to him. I laughed.

They took Stewie aside to talk to him. I could tell they were chewing him out. The officer told me if that would have happened in Utah they could have charged him with attempted murder. He advised me to get ahold of the police department in Wendover. I called them. I talked to an officer. They told me to write up what happened and email it to them. I did. I called to try to talk to someone several times. I could never reach anyone, so I just gave up.

I ran into Stewie a couple of times. We said hello. I'm glad to report that at this time he is clean and sober and I don't have anything to do with him.

Later that day Blane called me. I was crying when he called. He asked me what was wrong. I told him I was just having a bad day.

He said, "Bullshit. What's going on?"

I proceeded to tell him everything that had happened. He was more concerned with the fact that I had gotten a room with Stewie than about him possibly infecting me with HIV. Shouldn't have expected anything different. He was more concerned about me sleeping with someone than having a life-threatening disease.

I thought to myself it doesn't matter anyway. Where not going to be together. I was sure that the Parole Board and the probation department would put an end to our relationship.

Blane had asked me to contact this sex offender therapist that was involved with helping sex offenders with their rights. I wrote her a letter and told her our situation. She wrote me back and said that we would definitely not be allowed to see each other. Her reasoning was that we had broken his parole together. Plus, I still had minor children. So, I knew it was just a matter of time. She said we had slipped through the cracks with our being able to visit while he has been incarcerated, but once he was paroled, they would make sure we didn't have any contact.

Knowing that we were not going to be together, I felt that I shouldn't have to spend all the money I was spending driving to visit, phone call, and money on his books. So, I sold the red Chevy truck that he loved. We had gotten it at the auction and fixed it up. On a trip, we took to St. George we blew it up. We ended up parking it in my back yard until I sold it. He was pissed. I didn't care. I felt he deserved it. That was nothing compared to all the pain he had caused me. I guess in some ways I was intentionally hurting him.

He couldn't do anything about what I did while he was in jail.

THE STING

It was Labor Day weekend; my kids were at their Dad's for a family BBQ. Harmony called me and said her sister-in-law told her that there was a guy, staying with her Dad and that she got weird vibes from him, so she looked him up and found out that he was a sex offender. I told Harmony to get me his name.

On Tuesday, I pulled him up and sure as shit he was a predator. I know that my ex-husband's girlfriend would not be okay with him living a few feet away from her thirteen-year-old daughter. I knew that she didn't know.

I called Blane's old probation officer to tell him what I knew. I also told Blane what was going on. I didn't hear anything back

On my birthday, I was out to lunch with Joe. I went to use the bathroom, and for some odd reason, I decided to call the probation officer again. I talked to someone else that time. I explained to them how that little girl was not safe. He walks in and out of the house at his leisure. I ended up talking to a supervisor. I told him that I could deliver him right into their hands. I told them I could get him in my car and drive him where ever they wanted.

He said, "That would be too dangerous. How would we know what car was yours for sure?"

I said, "Check this out. I drive a Crossfire convertible, charcoal and the license plates say JULEEB. I would have the top down so you could see him in the car. You would have the address we are leaving from so someone could see us getting into the vehicle."

He said, "Let me call you back. I'm going to talk to someone about this."

About thirty minutes later I got a call back. They wanted me to help take him down. The officer asked me how I was going to get him to go with me. I said, "He and my ex-husband are using drugs. I'm a recovering addict, and I know how to act like I'm jonesing. I will tell him I need to score some coke. He will bite instantly thinking that he is going to be getting some."

He said, "We will call you back in a little while. We need to get everything set in place and then we will call you with the plan.

I said, "Awesome I will be waiting to hear from you." I was so excited my adrenaline was pumping hard. This guy had never done anything to hurt me, but he had hurt others. I know the kind of pain they felt from his actions, and I'm sure if they could have done something to get even with him they would.

Finally, the call came. The officer said, "Get him in your car. Drive to the Top Stop on 700 east and 2700 south. Pull up to the pump, turn your car off, take the key, get out and walk towards the store. We will call you and let your phone ring twice when were ready."

"Okay sounds good," I said.

I was at my ex-husband's house, sitting on the porch swing in his backyard. His girlfriend, her thirteen-year-old daughter, and Charlie were there. I didn't know Charlie. I talked to him for a few minutes. I had really bad cotton mouth from the excitement of what was about to unfold. I kept bouncing my leg and fidgeting. I wanted Charlie to think that I was high. He did. Then I asked him if he could score for me. He asked me what I wanted.

I said, "Crack or powder coke. Either one would be fine."

He said, "I can get you whatever you want."

I said, "That's awesome. Don't say anything to the ex. I don't want him to know that I have started using again. I will just say I'm going to get a drink. Then you just ask if you could ride along."

He said, "That sounds good to me."

A few minutes later my phone rang. It was in my purse, so I fumbled around inside my purse like I was trying to find it. I pulled it out and looked at it. I said, "It's my kid I'll call her back later." Then I put it back in my purse.

I waited about a minute stood up and said, "I'm going to get a drink anyone want one." On cue, he asked if he could go I said, "Sure."

We got in my car. My heart began beating fast. I began sweating; I could feel it running down my forehead. I was so excited about what was going to happen. I asked him if he had used any of the dope we were going to score?

He said, "Yes, it was really good, and I wouldn't be disappointed."

I thought to myself, well you sure will be. I told him I needed to stop to get a drink. We pulled into the Top Stop just like I was told to do. I got maybe two steps from the car when I was grabbed by the arm and dragged across the parking lot. As that was happening a lot of cops dressed in bullet proof vests, guns were drawn, ran up to the car. Several vehicles also came flying in, and cops jumped out.

The cop that had me was watching, and I said, "Officer you need to cuff me. I can't look like I had anything to do with this." He cuffed me, and I said, "My purse." He looked and saw that he had not taken it but left it hanging on my arm. He took off the cuffs, removed my purse and put the cuffs back on. He then started going through my purse.

After they had taken Charlie away, all the officers came over to where I was standing. The officer was taking off the handcuffs when this one cop walked up. He had an attitude.

He said, "So what's the deal with her." The officer in charge looked at him and said, "She's with us." He looked embarrassed and walked away. We continued to talk, and the officer in charge asked if I knew any other wanted felons. I said, "We'll I have this ex-husband."

He laughed and said, "Sorry I can't help you with that."

I was a glad that I was able to get this man away from that little girl. I'm sure it was only a matter of time before he would destroy her world. I just wish there was a way to save her from my ex-husband. He is also a predator but got away with it. There is no record of his crime. The lovely courts gave him a plea in abeyance for lude behavior. I was at least able to save her from one monster in her home.

I'M HERE

Joe's health began to decline. His family told me he couldn't be home alone.

I said, "I can come stay with him in the evenings, spend the night if someone can come relieve me in the morning so I can go to work."

We worked out a schedule. I would go to his house in the evening. He would be so glad to see me. He was not eating or drinking enough water so I would tell him that he would need to eat and drink if he wanted me to come back. Not fair I know but whatever it took to get him not to give up.

They decided to put him in an assisted living program. He asked me to be at the house when they started taking his things. They were going to sell the house; everything had to go. I told him, "I would be there."

Whenever Joe needed me to do something I would do it. He didn't have to ask twice. He made me feel wanted and loved so when he needed me I was there. I also loved him, so whatever he needed I would do.

Nights were really hard on both of us. He would get up several times a night. I would hurry to get out of bed to help him to the bathroom. Several times he didn't make it. He was so sweet. He would tell me, "He didn't need me to get up. That I needed my rest."

I would look at him smile and tell him, "I love you. I'm getting up, and you can't stop me. I will be here for you whether you like it or not."

He would smile at me, shake his head and say, "You're are so stubborn. I love you".

One evening while he was lying in my arms he said, "Honey I really thought that when I paid your house off, I would never see you again."

I said, "Joe haven't you figured it out yet? I love you, and I'm not going anywhere. I told you that in the beginning. It hasn't changed for me. I will be here until your final breath.

He said, "I'm so glad honey, I would be lost without you. You are my Julee."

I said, "Yes Joe I am and always will be."

I could tell he was starting to get uncomfortable. I helped him turn onto his side so could get comfortable and go to sleep.

I laid there with tears rolling down my cheeks. I could tell that he was getting weaker by the day. I knew I was going to lose him, and I dreaded that day.

Joe had picked the assisted living program that he was going to move to. He made sure that it was a place that would allow Russy to come live there as well.

Moving day was very stressful. I got there early so I could enjoy a cup of coffee with Joe before everyone got there. The day was full of surprises. I was sitting in the recliner chair when Joe told me to get the Bose stereo and put it in my car.

As I was walking through the living room with it, his daughter said, "I want that go put it in my car."

Joe said, "I gave that to Julee."

She was pissed. She stormed out the front door. I told Joe she could have it if she wants it.

He said, "No, I want you to have it."

There had been several times while we were preparing a meal that we would turn it on. On a couple of occasions, we would slow dance in the middle of the kitchen. I really enjoyed those weekends we would spend together.

His son asked me where the kitchen aide mixer was. I could tell by the way he asked me that he thought I had already taken it.

I said, "Oh that's downstairs right where it has always been. Let me go get that for you."

Joe instructed me to take the oval coffee table that was made out of a large piece of tree. It was a very pretty table that his grandson had made in wood shop. My granddaughter would sit at that table and eat her cereal. The two of us would color in her coloring books at that table. His other daughter wanted that, and once again he said, "No, I want Julee to have it." So, I loaded it in my car.

That table holds a lot of memories from my time living there.

We got a lot done that day and got Joe moved into his new place. I think his children finally came to realize that I was good for Joe. That I wasn't going anywhere, and no matter what they couldn't tear us apart. They started letting me know what was going on. If something happened, they would notify me.

HALFWAY HOUSE

It had been almost a year since I had visited Blane in Jail. They transferred him to Ogden county jail for the remainder of his sentence. At that jail, they allowed contact visits when they got close to release.

I wasn't sure how I was going to feel when he would hug me. It had been such a long time. I loved him, and I hated him. I had forgiven him for everything that he had done to me. It wasn't easy. I did a lot of praying, studying the Bible and I also went to a bible study every other week for a year.

We had written each other constantly throughout the year. In the letters, he would tell me how much he loved me. How sorry he was for hurting me. How things were going to be different and that he was going to make things right between us. I fell for it. I wanted to believe that he loved me. I believe that is what we all want. We just want to be loved, and many of us who stay in abusive relationships believe they love us. That no one else will.

You were allowed to bring dinner on your visit. I knew it had been a long time since he had a steak. I picked dinner up at the Long Horn. I got him all his favorites. I got there a little early and had to wait. It seemed like I was waiting forever.

They finally took me back to see him. He hugged me tightly. Tears began to roll down his cheeks. The officer said that's enough. We sat on the floor picnic style to eat our dinner. He said. "It felt so good to hold you. It has been so long."

I said, "It has been a long time."

I thought that I would feel happy when I finally got to give him a hug. I didn't feel anything. It wasn't a big deal. We ate our dinner. He kept saying he was sure they would let us be together. I told him that I didn't think that was going to happen. I really believed that they were going to step in and stop the relationship. That is what I was hoping.

Every time I would try to walk away he would manipulate me. He would call me nonstop. I would come back. I wasn't strong enough to just walk away on my own; I had tried countless times with no success.

They sent him to a halfway house that was only a few miles away from my house. He contacted me and told me he needed some things brought to him. I was shocked that they had let him call me.

I got the items that he needed and to took them down there. They let him sit in the lobby area and visit with me. I went back several times with the things he needed, and each time they let us visit. He would say it is God who is doing this for us. He brought us together, and he is making way for us to be together. I would scream in my head no this can't be so. He would not want me to be hurt the way you have hurt me.

A week before Christmas his caseworker at the halfway house told me that we weren't allowed to see or talk to each other anymore. At first, I was very angry. I couldn't stop crying. Blane kept calling me. I told him what she said. I told him not to call me anymore. I blocked the number so I wouldn't answer it when he called. He came by my house a couple of days later when he was going to work. I told him, he couldn't do this you're going to get into trouble. Once again, he was doing what he wanted to do. He never follows the rules he feels he is untouchable and can do whatever he wants.

He said, "Don't worry honey I will get things worked out."

I was so hoping that they would just keep it the way it was. I needed them to make our separation happen.

VA HOSPITAL

It was December 27th, and I was at work. I got a call from my sister. She was freaking out. She said, "I think Dad has had a stroke. He won't let me call an ambulance. He won't listen to me."

I told her, "I will be right over."

I gathered all of my cleaning supplies and told my client that I had to go.

I got to Dad's house, and he was very confused. I told him we were taking him to the hospital. I struggled to get his coat on him because he kept trying to put the wrong arm in the sleeve. I finally got it on him.

We walked out to the garage. He got in the driver's seat. I told him he was not driving. He kept trying to start the car. He didn't even have the key in his hand, but he still kept trying.

My sister told him a couple of times to get out of the car, but he wouldn't listen. I asked him once, and he didn't listen. I reached into the car. I grabbed him by the lapels of his Levi coat and yanked him out. I then lead him over to the side of the drive way as my sister backed the car out. I put him in the passenger seat and buckled him in. I got in the back seat.

We took him to an Instacare. They told us we need to take him to the VA.

They immediately admitted him when we got him to the hospital. After running a bunch of tests, they told us he had pneumonia. His confusion was due to lack of oxygen. We were also told that his COPD had gotten a lot worse. They gave him a week to maybe a month to live.

We were all devastated. Dad said he wanted to die at home.

While there I got a call from Joe's daughter. He had been admitted to the hospital. He was almost directly below Dad's room. I spent a couple of days running up and down the stairs, visiting both of them.

Joe stayed for a couple of days and then was sent home.

My sister and I put a plan together to take care of our Dad. I wasn't able to help out as much as her. I still had the kids at home and worked full time running my cleaning business. My sister moved in with mom and Dad. I would spend every other weekend at their house and Sunday so my sister could see her family. They were wrong at the hospital. He lived for another six months.

ALLOWED

Blane called me all excited telling me that they told him if my parents came down they would do the interview and have him do his disclosure, that they could become his sponsor. Blane had to have sponsors to go on pass.

My parents wanted to do it because they had grown to love him. I went to my parent's house and told them. They said they wanted to do it. My Dad was still struggling with his breathing. My mother could barely walk due to her having bad knees and fibromyalgia.

We got down to the center and found out that he misunderstood what they had said. My Dad was very upset. It took all he had to go down there and then to find out it was a waste of time.

My angel from the emergency room and her husband had gone out to Fillmore with me to visit him. We went to their house for a dinner party the night before he had been arrested. They were shocked. I had never told them about his background.

Once he was arrested, I told them everything about his past. But I didn't say anything about what he had been doing to me for the ten months I was with him. I was too embarrassed and ashamed. They knew that I still cared about him. They also believe that people make bad choices but can change. They believed he was a changed man. He had them fooled. He was good at making himself look like a good person while doing evil acts. They agreed to go through the process to be a sponsor. They were approved.

Then I got a call from Blane. He was in his counselor's office. The counselor wanted me to come in, so I scheduled an appointment with him.

When I arrived, Blane was sitting in the lobby. He got up and came over and gave me a hug and a kiss on the cheek. His counselor came out. He introduced himself and then had me follow him to an office. Blane followed behind us.

Once we were in there, he said he had heard a lot about me. He said, "All good of course." He told me that he would like me to come in for a few sessions. Once you do that I will approve you to be a sponsor. In my head, I'm screaming. What!!!! How can this be happening? I was counting on the system to jump in, but they didn't. They were allowing him to see me even though I had minor children. Even though I was the reason, he went back. It made no sense to me.

We went on a pass with my friends. We went to dinner and a concert. We had a great time. He opened doors for me. He was funny as usual. He could be so charming when he wanted to be.

They started letting me take him on passes. We spent most of his passes at my mom and Dads. We played a lot of Yahtzee with my Dad. It was the only thing Dad could do at this point.

We took the boat out on one of our passes. We also went on a bicycle ride on a trail. He seemed so different. He didn't push himself on me. He respected me when I told him I was tired and didn't want to have sex. Going back to jail had changed him. I know that he told me he was reading his Bible.

He said, "He had asked God to change him. To help him be a better person." It seemed if that were the case.

It all changed once he was out of the halfway house.

CELEBRATING JOE'S BIRTHDAY

My granddaughter and I went shopping for
Joe's birthday present. He had complained about
being cold. I thought a soft throw blanket would make
him happy. We also went to the grocery store and
bought him a blue cupcake that had a flag on it that
read Happy Birthday. We went down to his new
place. They had moved him from the assisted living
center to a place that provided more services.

When he was at his assisted living center, I
would have breakfast with him in the dining hall. He
would introduce me as his wife. When we would get
back to his apartment, we would talk and laugh about
how some of the people would react. It didn't bother
us. Neither one of us cared about what anyone else
thought.

My granddaughter and I took his gift and
cupcake to him. As soon as he saw her, he got a huge
smile on his face. She crawled up on to his lap, and he
wrapped his arms around her and kissed her on the
top of her head.

He began asking her about school. How she was doing. He loved her so much. She helped him unwrap his present. He couldn't take his eyes off her.

He said, "She is beautiful. Make sure to keep a close eye on her those boys are going to be chasing her." He told her how much he loved her and gave her a big hug when we left. Tears welled up in his eyes.

I think he knew that it was the last time he was going to see her.

DEATH COMES IN THREES

A few weeks after Joe's birthday, he began to decline. He didn't want to eat. I would visit him at meal time. They had him eating in a room with only a few other patients to watch just in case he choked on his food. I was able to get him to eat a little.

One afternoon when I arrived they had him on an exercise bike. He was refusing to cooperate. He was tired. He had told me several times that he was ready to go. He didn't want to fight anymore. He said, "Why do they want me to fight to get stronger. I'm old. I'm tired, and I have had enough."

So, on that day when he would not cooperate, I told them to take him off the bike. He doesn't want to do it. He looked at me and smiled. I don't know if it was because he was glad I was there or if it was because I stood up for him. Don't get me wrong Joe could stand up for himself but the fact that he knew I cared enough to say something made him happy.

I got a call from Joe's daughter; He had a stroke. I hurried down to his place. They had moved him from the room upstairs to a room where they had more staff available to meet his needs.

When I arrived, his kids were there. They told me things didn't look good. They were in the process of signing him up for hospice services. He didn't want anything to be done to prolong his life.

We all sat around and talked. They asked me how my Dad was doing. I really can't remember much about what we talked about. I just knew my heart was breaking. My best friend was going to be leaving me. I went home, and I cried most of the night. I called Blane to tell him what was going on. He knew that I had been seeing Joe. I wasn't going to hide it. I wasn't going to let him make me stop.

He said, "I'm sorry." That was it. Nothing more.

I went to see Joe the next day. I entered the room. Joe's son said, "Did you see that. Dad heard her voice. He tried to smile. He knows she is here."

I sat on the edge of his bed. I began talking to him, but there was no response. Maybe he just thought he saw something. I think he did see something. I believe Joe had been waiting for me to get there.

As we were all sitting there visiting. His daughter said, "We have decided that we want you to have Dad's chair. Joe's chair had moved with him everywhere he went. It was an extra-large, brown lazy boy. I had slept in that chair many nights when I was living at his house. On several occasions, he would tell me to sit on his lap. I would laugh and tell him I was too heavy. He would disagree with me. I would then sit on his lap. I remember how he would cuddle with my granddaughter in that chair. It touched my heart so much when they told me they wanted me to have it. My eyes welled up with tears, but I quickly choked them back. I didn't want them to see how much it meant. I told them, "Thank you."

A short time later his son and one of his daughters left. His daughter Deedee, and I stayed.

They came in and gave Joe his Morphine. Deedee had decided to go try to find the doctor. I sat on the edge of Joe's bed and took his hand into mine. I told him how much I loved him. How he had changed my life in so many ways. How he had shown me what the true meaning of love was. How wonderful he is. I began to cry as I was telling him all these things. I then told him it was okay to let go. It's time for you to go live with God. That his wife was there waiting to be reunited with him.

Once I was done telling Joe everything I prayed to God to release him. To bring him home. I thanked God for giving me the opportunity to have such a wonderful man in my life. After I was done praying I began to sing to Joe. He loved it when I sang. He always said I had the voice of an angel. I sang the first verse of amazing grace. I hadn't quite finished when he crossed to the other side. Tears began rolling down my cheeks; I laid my head on his chest and began sobbing.

I left the room to find Deedee. She was heading towards the room. I approached her; I told her that her Dad had passed. She hurried into the room. She began to cry. I wrapped my arms around her. I told her how sorry I was. I said, "Your Dad loved you so much."

I came back several hours later to get the chair because I didn't trust these kinds of places. They always seem to lose things. I thought that they would have had things done before I returned. I was amazed that they were just getting around to bathing him. I sat there as they were cleaning him up. I suddenly had an overwhelming feeling of joy. I knew he was in the presence of God, that he was with his bee. He was no longer in pain.

Joe A. French 4-13-1928 to 5-18-2015. Like I said he was a lot older than me. I was forty-six, he was eighty-four when we got married.

I went straight to my Dad's. I told him that Joe and had passed.

He said, "That lucky son of a bitch. I wish it had been me." Dad was starting to struggle a lot. He couldn't make it up the stairs to play Yahtzee anymore. The last few times we did play he would get very upset because he would get confused on the adding or what he needed to get to put on his card. He was angry most of the time, and neither I or my sister could do anything right. He had me in tears several times as well as my sister. We took it in stride because we knew that he was struggling.

Two days after Joe died my sister called me; crying and upset. I can't wake Dad up. I immediately left my job and went to Dad's. His oxygen level was low. We called the nurse to have her come out and access the situation. She said, "He is on the decline. All you can do is try and keep him comfortable."

He finally woke up but was very confused. He wanted to go to the bathroom. We told him he couldn't walk there. He began fighting us to get up and go. We gave in, and the two of us helped him to the restroom. It was extremely difficult. We talked afterward, and both agreed. We can't do that again. I stayed there for the next several days. My sister and I kept taking turns on his meds. He began to have the rattling breathing sound that comes when a person in nearing the final stage of life.

I knew Dad was going to be passing over. I told Blane that I didn't think he was going to make it through the night. At five in the morning, Blane stopped by before going to his job. He was still in his halfway house and once again breaking the rules. He was driving his own truck when he was not allowed to have a vehicle. He was coming over here when he did not have permission. I told him he needed to go inside and tell Dad goodbye because he wasn't going to last much longer.

He went inside followed behind him. Dad needed to be changed because he had soiled himself. Blane and I changed Dad's diaper. I then left the room to give Blane time alone with him so that he could tell him goodbye. Blane came up the stairs with tears streaming down his face. He gave me a hug. I walked him to his truck. He said, "Keep me posted."

I said, "I will."

We hugged each other. He then got into his truck and headed to work.

I went inside. My sister was downstairs with Dad. I went down there. We just sat there for a few minutes in silence looking at Dad. It was time for his medication. It was my turn to give it to him. I gave it to him. I checked his oxygen level, and it was really low. The rattling sound had gotten significantly louder. I knew that it was time for me to tell him goodbye.

I said, "I love you, Dad. I know I didn't get to spend my childhood with you, but I have been blessed to have gotten to know you as an adult. I'm really going to miss you. I wish we could have done more together. I know that you are tired. It's okay for you to go. God is waiting for you."

I prayed to God as soon as I was done telling Dad goodbye. I asked him to open his arms and let him come home. I told him that he is tired and has suffered long enough. I grabbed Dad's hand and told him I would be lying down just a few feet away. I laid down on the floor. I just stared at the ceiling. I just could not watch another person I loved leave me.

I must have dozed. His dog Toby began barking; I got up and went to his bedside. He was gone. He had passed over into a better place. I began to cry, then walked upstairs to tell my sister. She began crying as well. Then I had to go up and tell mom. She began to cry. She put on her robe and went downstairs to be near Dad.

I was standing in front fo the kitchen sink looking out the window. My phone rang. I looked at it. I thought to myself. This is weird; my favorite client never gets up this early. I answered it.

She told me that Claudia had died a few hours ago. I began crying again. No not another. I had just seen Claudia the week before. I knew she didn't have long. She had been dealing with cancer for many years. It had finally taken her. I was able to tell her I loved her and what a wonderful woman she was. We gave each other a big hug because we both knew that it was going to be the last time we saw each other.

I was numb; I lost three people I love in one week. I just wanted to scream. To break things. To just run. I was angry. I was lost.

I knew in my heart that it was the best thing for all of them. It was still hard though because I didn't have them anymore.

I called Blane and told him that Dad had passed. He said he was going to call the center to see if they would let him leave work to help me. They granted him a five-hour pass to be with us at the house.

I left to go pick him up. While I was gone, the mortuary came to pick up Dad's body. I was really glad I wasn't there for that.

A few days after Dad died I heard that my step-mother had given her daughter some of his things. I was pissed. How could she do that? Dad said his things belonged to me and my sister Tina. I went over to mom's house to find out what she had given away. She had given Chris some of his Eagles.

While I was there, I overheard, my mom, telling someone on the phone that she was going to give some stuff to her son. It made me furious. How could she give my Dad's stuff to her children? He made it clear before he died that it went to Tina and me.

I began boxing up his stuff. Tina had asked me to do it. She wanted to spend some time at home because she had been living at Dad's house for the last six months.

We were at mom's house one Saturday afternoon. The yard needed to be mowed, so Blane got out the regular lawn mower and began mowing the lawn. My step-sister, myself and my mom were sitting on the front porch. I realized that the lawn mower sounded the same for a long time.

I got up and walked over to the side of the house where Blane was with the mower. He was just standing there staring across the street. I looked over to see where he was staring. There were two little girls, having a lemonade stand. He realized I was standing there and began to push the mower. I was really concerned with what I had just witnessed. It sent chills down my spine.

As we were leaving, he looked over at them and waved. I said, "What are you doing? You're not supposed to have any kind of contact with children."

He said, "Whatever Julee, I just waved at them. There is nothing wrong with that."

I didn't say anything else. It would just end up in a big fight.

As soon as we got home, he was all over me. I think watching those little girls had aroused him. He was not going to take no for an answer.

Blane took Dad's riding lawn mower. He said that Dad had told him he could have it if he took care of the yard. My step sister Chris called him late one night and told him to return it. He immediately called my mom. He was telling her Dad gave it to him. He was very intimidating. I was laying there, thinking you liar. He never said that. She told him he could have it. My step-sister was having no part of that. She wanted it back. Blane tried to get me to say that Dad said that. I told him I wasn't going to do it and I didn't.

My nephew came to the house and picked it up. Blane stood in the yard and talked with my nephew. I was really glad that there was no arguing or fighting. Blane has not spoken to or seen my mother since. It is really sad that something as stupid as a material object can destroy a relationship. My mother really loved Blane.

On several occasions, I talked to my mom when he was in prison about leaving him. She would tell me not to. He loves you. Everyone makes mistakes. She didn't know anything about what he had been doing to me. I know that if she did she would have wanted me to leave him.

THE HOUSE

Dave Blane's Dad called me. He said, "There is a house, two doors down from one of my rentals that is for sale. You should take a look. It would be a great investment property."

I drove by the house he mentioned. I wrote down the number. I told Blane about it. We went over and looked at it when he was on a pass that weekend. We both fell in love with it. His Dad told me about it because he knew Blane didn't have any money. He knew it would be me who was investing my money.

We contacted the owner. We met with him, and explained Blane's situation, but didn't tell him what his charges were. He probably wouldn't have sold the house to us if he knew. He said he would work with us. I purchased a five-thousand-dollar cashier's check with both of our names on it as the earnest deposit. It wouldn't go through because I had the money put away and not in the bank. We had to ask his Dad to help us.

His Dad gave him a check. He said it was a gift, but took my five thousand. We had to show a money trail. I was pissed about that. I felt like they were trying to play me. I felt that his Dad should have put it as a gift to both of us.

When we were trying to finance the house my debt to income was too high. I told Blane I wanted to sell the boat. I paid his friend Mindy a lot of money to help me clean it so I could put it up for sale. I asked Blane multiple times to help me list it. He just kept blowing me off.

It never got listed. In the end, I was not on the house loan, but he did put me on the title. I made sure of that. It was a very long process. The owner allowed us to move in before things were final. He gave us a house full of furniture, broken down car, dishes, tools, BBQ, tile, and a lot of other things.

I never felt like it was my home. Blane put all of his clothes in the two bedrooms upstairs and made me put mine in the basement. He wouldn't allow the dogs in the house.

When winter came, and it was freezing cold, I would beg him to let me bring them in. He wouldn't let me. My kids were angry with me because they were kept outside. I told his sister, and she even tried to convince him to let them in.

He finally gave me permission to bring them in. I ran to Costco and bought them big beds to put in the den. At night, I would put them down in the laundry room. He made sure that if they barked he would elbow me or yell your dogs are barking. He wouldn't help me with them in any way.

Tiffany suffered in that house as well. If she pooped our peed in the house, he would spank her so hard that she would yelp for a long time after. I would hurry home to try and find her accidents and clean them up before he saw them. I started keeping her in the bathroom so she wouldn't get punished.

One day she had pulled all the toilet paper down off the roll. I thought it was cute that she had amused herself by playing in it. I showed Blane. He didn't think it was cute at all and spanked her really hard. I told him to stop. He told me I needed to start disciplining her or I would have to get rid of her. I felt horrible. I didn't know he was going to do that to her. I picked her up. I hugged her close to me and told her how sorry I was. I did everything I could to protect her.

He didn't seem to care at his Dad's place, but I guess his home meant more to him. Just goes to show how your things are more important to you than the things that belong to someone else.

MY BOY

I took Bennett to his Dad's house to spend some time with him. He didn't want to go. He never wanted to go over there because he didn't like his Dad. His Dad was always too busy to give him any attention. He was either working on his pond or the hot rod. I made him go over there anyways hoping that his Dad would give him the attention he needed.

His Dad lets him drive the golf cart up and down the street. Bennett decided to take off in it. He didn't come back. I had to call and report him as a runaway again. His Dad and grandparents called the police and reported the golf cart stolen.

I began looking for Bennett.

On one Sunday, I dressed up in a wig, ugly floral shirt, tan kaki's pants, boots and a hat. I went to Liberty Park where they held drum circles. It just so happened they were having a car show that weekend. Bennett's Dad and his girlfriend were there with his hot rod. I walked around his car, stood next to him and his girlfriend during the awards ceremony. They didn't recognize me at all. I even went up to the stand my car insurance lady had set up. I browsed through her pamphlets. She asked me if I wanted some information. I said, "No thank you." I looked her directly in the face, and she didn't recognize me either.

I walked over to the area where they had a drum circle. A drum circle is where they have people playing drums. The people that attend are usually smoking pot and just hanging out. It's really just a party they say it's a religious thing. I walked around looking for Bennett. I asked a couple that was sitting with their dogs if I could sit with them. I told them what I was doing and showed them his picture.

Harmony called me and wanted to know where I was. She said I will be right over. I watched her as she walked around looking for me. She walked past me twice. She finally called me and said, "I can't find you." She was standing about 15 feet in front of me looking right in my direction. I told her to look straight. Do you see those big dogs? Go over to that group of people. She walked up. I said, "Hi."

She said, "Oh my God!!! I couldn't tell that was you."

I dressed up like that on several other occasions. I wanted to find my boy. I worried about him constantly.

Harmony and I went down to Fairmont park looking for him. We saw a group of kids. As we were walking towards them, one of the kids got up and left. We thought it might be Bennett but weren't quite sure. We asked the group if it was him. They said, "No."

Harmony said I will give whoever tells me the truth ten dollars. One of the kids said, "Yes, It's him."

Harmony yelled his name and took off running towards him. He started running. I started running while trying to call 911. I had kicked off my sandals because they were slowing me down. Then I came upon a lot of broken glass. I had to go around it.

Bennett ran under the underpass and up the side of the hill. He was hiding in the bushes. Harmony came up behind him and wrapped her arms around his torso. He flipped her forward. She went face first into the rocks. He took off running.

All I could see when I caught up with them, was the back of him running down the street. Harmony had cuts all over her legs and her face. She had glass in her feet. She ran straight through all that glass.

We drove around for quite a while after that looking for him. We knew it was a lost cause and finally gave up and went home. I did finally get a hold of someone at 911, but it was too late.

Bennett, eventually go arrested. He had a whole bunch of new charges. When they called me the night he was picked up they asked if I wanted to talk to him. I said, "No." I was trying to do the tough love thing. I really wanted to hear his voice. I had missed him and been so worried.

I didn't see him on the first visiting day. I wanted him to think that he had burned the bridge. That maybe that might make him want to change his behavior. I couldn't stay away. Blane told me I should not visit him at all. But I couldn't do that. He is my son. I need to be there for him.

We went to court, and they ordered him into another program. He has done a lot of programs. I went to all the visits. Took him on all the passes they gave him. I was not going to abandon him.

OUT OF THE HALFWAY HOUSE

Before Blane could be released from his program, the Parole Department had to approve the place where he was going to reside. Blane asked me to meet his new parole officer at his Dad's shop. He had to work and couldn't be there.

I met his new Parole officer and his partner. I showed them around. Then he asked me why Blane was violated. I proceeded to tell him about our relationship. How we had hidden it from them. He gave me a disapproving look. His partner just stood back and observed our, interaction. He was gorgeous. He had the most beautiful eyes. I thought to myself too bad he is not his parole officer. They approved the apartment which we knew they would, considering he had lived there before.

Blane got out of the halfway house in June 2015. He moved back into his Dad's apartment above the shop. He wanted me there all the time. Bennett was gone, and Harmony had her boyfriend, so I started staying at his apartment.

I went with Blane to his first appointment with his Parole Officer. They pulled my sponsorship; I was no longer allowed to take him on activities.

I got upset and stormed out of the office. I thought great now what are we going to do. We will be trapped in that apartment, and I knew what that would intel. The thought of that just made me cringe. They changed his parole officer. My wish had come true; he got the cute one.

Larry was very direct. He said he would not have given us permission to see each other, but because they approved it in the halfway house, he was going to go with that. He said that my status as a sponsor was suspended, but after time and with his therapist approval it could be reinstated. I went with Blane to all of his appointments. It never was.

As part of his release from the halfway house, he was ordered to do therapy. I went with him to his therapy appointments; it was a joke. I would sit there, session after session, and watched him lie to him.

At his sexual evaluation, Blane sat there and lied. I was screaming inside. His therapists asked him how often he needed sex. Blane said, "Like two times maybe three times a week."

I was screaming inside liar. You want it every night and in the morning.

He asked him how often he thought about it. He said, "Not that often really."

I wanted to say bullshit. I watched him when we went to the store or anywhere in public. He would look at women, and I could see him undressing them in his mind. His whole facial expression would change. He would see that I was watching him and look away. He wanted and needed sex all the time.

If I said the wrong things in the sessions, he would tell me after we left, that I have to watch what I say. It could cause problems for us.

His relationship, with his therapist, was more life-friends; he had his therapist totally manipulated, he believed everything Blane told him.

MOVING IN

We moved into the new house in August 2015. We had to jump through hoops to get it financed. Blane didn't close on it for a couple of months. The owner allowed us to move in while things were being done to qualify. I told Blane on several occasions that I didn't want to do it. I just wanted my five thousand back. He said it was too late we had already given it to the owner. I was afraid that he was going to burn me on it. In essence, he has up to this point. I'm not on the loan, but I am on the title. I hope someday to get this situation resolved, but at this point, I have decided to leave it alone.

The house has four bedrooms. Two upstairs and two in the basement. The front yard has beautiful flower beds all across the front and a flagpole on the east side of the front yard, and it's brown brick.

We always entered through the back door. When you go into the back door, you are in the family room. There are windows that line the whole north wall. To the right of the door; two steps that go up into the kitchen. The kitchen has beautiful handmade cabinets that the owner had made himself. The kitchen floor was hard wood.

As you leave the kitchen, you go into the living room. There are two windows directly in front and one on the side. After entering the living room, there is an opening where the hall is. On the left side of the hall is the bathroom; it was gorgeous, all tile, I loved it.

Next, to the bathroom, there was a staircase that led to the basement. Next, to that, there were two bedrooms. We used the one that faced the street. Blane used the closet in that room and the bedroom next to us.

At the bottom of the basement stairs on the left, was the laundry room. It had a toilet, counter with a sink and a shower that had not been finished. Across from the laundry room was another room. Blane made that into his office. Next to that was another bedroom.

I always had to go down there to get clothes to shower. I asked him many times if we could make room for my stuff upstairs. He would just ignore me. He also had all of his stuff in the garage. In the far backyard behind the dog kennels, there was a room. That's where he let me put some of my stuff.

I began to resent him more and more. He made me feel like I was worth nothing. Like I had no interest in the home. Like I didn't belong.

OFF TO CALIFORNIA

My sister Tina, and I took off in June to California to visit family. We wanted to take our brothers their Dad's ashes, and an Eagle from his collection. Tina and I had grown close during our ordeal with Dad.

Blane was not happy about me going, but I didn't care. I was going.

I went to a lot of places from my past while I was in California. I went up to Big Bear where my brothers were still living. We all got together and had a BBQ. It was so nice getting to know my nieces and nephews. The youngest of my nieces attached herself to me.

I drove over to my mother's old house, it didn't look like I remembered. The new owners had totally remodeled it. I was overjoyed when I saw that they hadn't cut down the pine tree that I had given her for Christmas in 1994. I just stood there and looked at the tree remembering all the times I had come to visit. It had been a long time since I had been there.

I went to Compton to see Mrs. Talker and the whole family. I hadn't seen them in years. We had lost contact, and I didn't know where anyone lived. One evening while I was lying in bed I decided to try and find them. I searched Facebook until I found one of the kids, I was so excited. I messaged him hoping that it was him. I was sure that it was because he looked just like I remembered. He hadn't changed a bit.

Once I knew it was him, I told him that Tina and I were coming down for a visit. I asked him to not tell his mom that I had found them. I found his sister on his friends list and added her.

We arranged a surprise get to together at Shelley's hair shop. They didn't tell Mrs. Talker anything about us. We got to the shop. Mrs. Talker hadn't arrived yet. She lived in the apartment building right across the street. We hid in the kitchen area when we saw that Mrs. Talker was crossing the street. All the others were just sitting around the salon.

When she walked in and was in the middle of the room Tina, and I walked out of the kitchen. Mrs. Talker opened her arms wide. She had tears in her eye. She said, "Juleekay." I hurried over, and she wrapped her arms around me.

I felt like I was home. I love her so much. She was always there for me when my mother wasn't. She was more like my mom than my own mom. We spent several hours just visiting and reminiscing about the old days. We took lots of pictures.

Shelley and I went for a drive in my little Sports car. We spent the night at Shelley's house. She only lived a block from the house I lived in when I was 5. The park and school were still there.

They had put a fence to separate the school from the park. My sister and I walked around the school and the park. We had to stay on the sidewalk because it was fenced off. We stopped at the side of the school. The bungalows were still there. The school hadn't changed a bit. I stood there and stared at the two buildings where that girl had taken me. I wanted to cry, but I didn't because my sister was standing there. She asked if I was alright. I looked at her smiled and said, "Yeah I'm fine. Let's go." I wasn't fine.

I walked over to the house I lived in. I stood at the end of the driveway. I started remembering the day that my mother and big brother where beating the crap out of the family station wagon with bats. They were yelling all kinds of profanities. I just stood there frozen, starring not knowing why they were doing that. My mother would just go insane sometimes screaming and yelling.

I also saw the fire hydrant that my stepfather fell into head first when he was running after me. He was trying to stop me from running into the street. It broke his neck, but luckily it didn't cause permanent damage. I was only five at the time of these incidents. It was also right around the same time I was molested at the school. I wanted to go back to these places so that I could have closure. I needed to face the demons that have been in my head.

We went to downtown Long Beach, to the hotel I lived in with Brett. I stood on the street and looked up at the window where are the room was. The big hotel sign was covered with a tarp. The front doors were no longer there. They had moved the entrance to the side of the building. I closed my eyes, and I could hear the screams. That last Fatal night came rushing back in.

I began crying and then sobbing. I hadn't been back her since 1984.

Blane called me. He could tell that I was crying. I told him where I was. He asked if I was alright. I said, "No." I told him I had to go and would call him later. What happened that night changed my life forever. I want to tell you more; but I can't.

We drove around the neighborhood where we grew up. Dominguez had changed some, but some places like Rob's liquor store and Carson market hadn't changed a bit. We even found the house that my great grandmother had lived in. Tina said it still looked the same. I was too young to remember that house.

We had an awesome trip. It was great spending time together remembering the good times. I was glad that I had Tina there with me when we went to the places where I had experienced such heartache. I hope to be able to make a trip with her again.

While I was gone, he called me and asked if he could hang out with my niece. He said he was asking because he didn't want us to have any problems. I said, "Yes." I trusted my niece. I thought that I could trust him seeing's how he asked me. We'll I shouldn't have.

He made several passes at her. He told her she didn't know what she was missing. She shot him down. She told him that she was going to tell me. He said, "She won't believe you."

She told me a few weeks after I was back about how he kept calling her. He even went as far as telling her if she played her cards right he would fix up the car in the backyard for her. That sent her over the edge. She called me and told me everything.

I confronted Blane, and he called her a liar. "She is just unhappy with her life and doesn't want to see anyone else happy. You can't believe anything that comes out of her mouth she is just a tweaker."

I did believe her because I know what kind of person he was.

THREESOME

Blane had to get a sponsor when he got out of the halfway house. If he didn't, we would not be able to do anything. He asked his best friend Mindy if she would be willing to become his sponsor. They had been friends for 30 plus years. She said she would.

She was still in denial of his crime. She didn't believe that he had done it. She felt that he had been railroaded by his ex and the system. I told her that wasn't true. He was guilty of the crimes. I don't know if she believed me.

The three of us started doing everything together. We went to a concert, boating, and the movies. She and Blane began doing work on my house so that I could get it ready to rent out. He was dragging his feet on it.

He told me that I needed to pay him for all the work he had done in my house before he went back to prison. He also informed me that I had to pay him for anything he did now. I was pissed. I thought he had done that for me because he was my boyfriend. I thought that when you're in a relationship you do things like that for each other. I did a lot of things for him and didn't expect payment.

Mindy did a lot of the work. I didn't have a problem with paying her. She did a good job. She was always working hard when I was there.

I got them several side jobs; that paid good money. He showed no appreciation. It was like he expected that. I began to feel like the third wheel. They played and joked around all the time. One day I decided I wanted to play too. They had been teasing each other with the paint brushes. I started to play with Blane the same way later that day. I got a little bit of paint on him, and he started yelling at me. It hurt, my feelings were crushed. I started to cry. How come it's OK for her and not me?

His mother called as I was sitting on the porch. Blane said, "I need to call you back, I just hurt Julee's feelings." He tried to hug me.

I pushed him away and said, "I will never try to play with you again."

He said, "Whatever." Then he walked into the house. I was jealous of their relationship. They seemed like they should be together. Some people had even commented to me that they thought they were in a relationship.

began to feel like a servant. He expected me to cook dinner. He would wait for me to bring it into him and Mindy while they were watching TV. When I would get up to go back in the kitchen, he would say, "Are you forgetting something?"

He was talking about the dishes.

Mindy did wash them for me on a couple of occasions. Blane began to refer to himself as the puppet master. He would call me his puppet. I would tell him, I'm not your puppet and he would say, "Yes you are. You do what I say and when I say."

He was right I had become his puppet. It made me so angry every time he would say it. It reminded me of what a loser I had become. I had allowed myself to fall back into that miserable existence. I had become very depressed. I hated my life. I hated everyone and everything. I went on Facebook and told everyone how much I hated them. I didn't want anybody in my life. I shut everyone out. I mean everyone but Blane. I shut him out emotional. I was only there physically.

I began to sleep a lot. I would go home from work and climb into bed. Mindy seemed to always come by when I was laying down. She would tell Blane. He began picking fights with me. He said I was lazy; I needed to clean the house more.

I just didn't have it in me. I paid my employee and Harmony to clean it. I didn't feel like it was even my home. He made all the rules.

His old behavior had returned. It was worse than before because I was going through menopause which made sex, extremely painful. That didn't matter to him. He would keep going until he got his climax.

On a couple occasion's he stopped. He would make me feel horrible about it. I hated it when that would happen because he would come back at me a couple of hours later to finish. I would wish that he would just get finished the first time so I wouldn't have to endure another assault.

t didn't happen in the shower anymore the water at the new house got cold really fast. We would jump in; hurry and wash and get out before it got cold. That didn't stop it from happening when we went to bed. I would tell him I didn't want to do it and he would say, "You never want to."

Then, of course, he would go at me anyways. There was a picture of Jesus hanging on the wall on his side of the bed. I would just stare at that picture the whole time. Praying to God to help me get out; asking him to do for me what I couldn't do for myself. I know he was there and I know he could hear me.

I got to a point where I thought I was going to explode. I needed to talk to someone. I had pushed everyone away.

I called my step sister Chris. I unloaded all my anger that I was holding onto about my Dad. I was angry and bitter. My Dad had commented on several occasions that he had paid my mother child support. Why would he not pay an attorney instead of giving her child support? How could he leave me with her? Knowing the kind of life, I was having to live. I didn't tell Chris about what Blane had been doing.

I was still hiding that from everybody.

BROKEN HEARTED

Joe had purchased our wedding bands at a store in the mall. He didn't like the way my band looked so he went back to that jeweler.

They wouldn't give him a refund but they did give him a store credit. He took me there and told me to find what I wanted. I wanted a cross. We sat there for over an hour looking through the books until I found the one I wanted. It was beautiful. It was a large gold cross with Jesus on it. He was white gold. We bought a nice strong chain for it. I put that cross on. I told Joe I would never take it off.

After Joe died I would place my hand on that cross every day. I would immediately think of him. I would even talk to him. I would tell him how much I missed him.

One evening I was coming home from visiting Bennett in his program, I went to touch my cross, it was gone. My heart hit the floor. Oh, my God where is my cross. I began sobbing. The chain was still around my neck but the cross was gone. I felt like my heart was being ripped from my chest. I loved that cross. Why? Not just because Joe had given it to me. It also represented my love for my Savior.

When I got home I found Blane and Mindy sitting outback on the patio. I walked up to them. I was still crying. Blane asked me what was wrong. I told him I had lost my cross. I began sobbing. He said, "Have you thought about where you could have lost it?"

I said, "I have no idea where I could have lost it or when."

He said, "You'll find it." Then went back to talking to Mindy.

A couple of days later, Mindy mentioned that we were looking at the porcelain dolls I was giving her in the driveway. Then I remembered how I had made the comment that the nun doll had a cross just like mine. I remember touching my cross. It was the next day that I noticed it was gone.

I went over to that spot and began searching for it. I didn't find it.

I asked Mindy if she would look in the doll container for me. I asked several times. I also asked Blane to ask her. I began getting angry. They were both ignoring my request. Then I got the excuse that the box was under a bunch of her stuff at her house. She finally told me that she had searched the container. It wasn't in there.

We took Blane's cousin Marten, and his girlfriend to my house. They were looking for a place to rent. They wanted to do the work on the house as part of the move in. We wanted to show them what we were doing. We walked them around the whole house. The next day my house was robbed.

I was devastated. The Eagle necklace my Dad had given me was in it. My great grandmother's diamond watch, my wedding ring that I got from Joe; cash and some other jewelry.

I called the police, and made a police report. I called the insurance company. They gave me the run around. I had mentioned Blane had been at the house. They found out he was a felon. I had also mentioned that my son had been in trouble. They wanted us to come in and meet with an attorney. I said screw it. I wasn't going to go through all this crap.

I'm so glad that I didn't. I went to my safety deposit box to get some papers a few months later. My grandmother's watch and the wedding ring were in there. I was so happy. At least I hadn't lost those. I just wish the gold Eagle my Dad had given me had been there but unfortunately it wasn't.

I never found my cross. I still reach for it on occasion. I'm going back to that jeweler and order the same one. It might not be the original cross Joe gave me but it will still remind me of him every time I hold it between my fingers.

SUPERPRISE SURPRISE SURPRISE

I hired a new lady to clean with me. Her name was Sapphire; she was a jewel. She went to Wendover a lot. She invited me to go several times. I always said no. I knew Blane wouldn't let me. One day in the shower I told Blane that she had asked me to go. He gave me a disapproving look, which let me know that it was not something he was going to let me do. I really wanted to go; so, I devised a plan.

My birthday was coming up in September. I told Sapphire that she needed to talk to Blane. I told her to tell him that he should plan a surprise birthday party for me. She should tell him that she will take me to Wendover for the night, and when we get home, he can have a party waiting for her. He went for it.

She pretended she was taking me to dinner when we were really going to Wendover. I played along knowing what we were doing. We laughed our asses off. My whole family knew what was going on. I even told my niece who he hated at this point because of what had happened at the beginning of summer to come to the party.

We returned home, and I went in the backyard. He had it decorated so beautifully. He went all out. He had bought a lot of food for the barbecue. None of my friends were there because he only told them about the party once weeks before. They had forgotten about it. I was upset at first but then realized that he hadn't followed through. I immediately started drinking. It didn't take me long to become drunk.

guest had brought some weed. I went out to the back and got stoned. I was sitting on the patio, Ali and her boyfriend were sitting in front of me. They were both talking to me at the same time. I felt like I was watching a talk show, the way they kept going back and forth. I was laughing inside because I couldn't understand a thing they were saying. I think they were trying to help me not feel bad about my friends not being there. I didn't feel bad. I was actually feeling really good.

Harmony and Blane had a big blow out. Blane had some of Harmony's boyfriend's tool and didn't want to give them back. Harmony started calling him a pedophile, rapist and a womanizer. She was yelling these things at the top of her lungs. She hated Blane. She was only putting up with him because of me.

I was so wasted I had to ask Blane to help me to the bathroom. I wrapped my around him and told him, thank you so much for the party. I was actually laughing on the inside.

It worked out for Sapphire as well. Her daughter's birthday was coming up; I gave her all the decorations for the party.

Blane still doesn't know to this day that I had planned the whole thing. I guess he will know now if he reads this book. I can only imagine how pissed he is at this moment.

HELD DOWN

On September 27th. When we went to bed that night, he said good night and gave me a kiss. He rolled over on his side to go to sleep. I continued to watch TV for a few minutes. Then I turned off the TV rolled onto my side and went to sleep.

In the middle of the night, Blane rolled over and climbed on top of me. I told him to stop, get off of me. He used his knee to force my legs apart. I placed my hands on his shoulders and tried to push him off of me.

I said, "No stop. Get off of me. I don't want to do this."

He ignored my plea. He took my wrists and placed my arms above my head and held them there. He forced himself inside of me. It hurt so bad. It was dry. I could feel myself ripping. Tears were rolling down my face.

I turned my head to the left and stared at Jesus. I began pleading with him to make this stop. Blane finished. He rolled onto his side and went back to sleep. I got out of bed. I stood in front of the stove just staring at it. I couldn't stop crying. I told myself you have to do something. You need to leave. I can't live like this anymore.

I eventually went back to bed. I didn't want to face him when he got up. His alarm went off. I acted like I was still asleep. He came over to me before he left and gave me a kiss goodbye and said have a good day.

What the hell? How can he act like that after what he just did to me? He held me down while I fought it. Of course, he never felt like he did anything wrong all the other times he took it or wouldn't stop.

I needed to talk to someone. I couldn't deal with this on my own anymore. I called my friend Mark.

Mark knew Blane from prison. I had gotten to know him while he was helping at my house. He lived a couple of blocks over, and when he would see me at the house, he would stop to visit. I called me as soon as Blane had left.

Mark said he would meet me at my house. I hurried over. I couldn't stop crying as I told him what happened. He told me I needed to report it. I told him I couldn't. He said that he had never liked Blane. I really should get away from him. He said I deserved better.

After Mark had left, I got out a pen and paper and wrote down everything that happened. I still had my room set up at my house. I hid the notebook between my mattresses.

I went over to Sheryl's house. The minute she saw me she knew something was wrong. She hugged me, and I began sobbing. I told her what happened. I sat in the chair at the table, and I pulled up my sweat pants up past my knees to show her the red marks he had left from forcing my legs apart. I canceled work that day, and I stayed at her house, and I slept all day.

Sheryl called the rape crises hotline. She didn't give them any names. She told me that I needed to contact them. I needed to turn him in. I told her I couldn't. I told her not to tell anyone. She said she would keep my secret. She told me she would be there for me no matter what I decided to do.

I walked around in a funk for a long time. I started spending a lot of time at Sheryl's. If I didn't have work, I would tell Blane I did. I would then go over to Sheryl's house. I would visit for a bit. Then I would climb into her bed. I always felt so safe and at peace when I was in her bed. I would sleep so soundly. I wouldn't sleep at home. I was always afraid that he would do the same thing he had done that night.

One day when I went down to get into Sheryl's bed, there was a teddy bear on it with a note that said, "Julee, I love you, and I'm here for you no matter what." I started bawling. I felt blessed to have such a wonderful friend.

I went to the doctor because I was having bladder leakage problems. She recommended surgery. She told me that I could not have intercourse for six weeks after. If I did, it could cause major damage and future problems. I knew he wouldn't let me go six weeks without sex.

I decided that I couldn't have the surgery.

SEEKING HELP

I decided that I need to find a therapist. I needed help; I wanted out. I figured I could get help working through things. I could get some confidence and self-esteem. That maybe that would help me to leave.

I talked to my therapist about things that were going on but led her to believe that I was talking about my past. I didn't want her to know what was really going on. I was afraid that she would report it.

She diagnosed me with PTSD. I have already been diagnosed with bi-polar disorder, border line personality disorder, and when I was eighteen, they said I was schizophrenic. I'm not Schizophrenic it was the drugs I was on that made it appear that way. The other diagnoses are correct. That therapist really helped me. I have had a lot of therapy throughout my life, and not one of the therapist realized that I had PTSD.

I hated lying to her. I wish I could just tell her that all this stuff is happening to me now. I did talk about some of the things that happened in the past. I talked to her about my kids. How I had abandoned them for men. How I had made so many bad choices. I saw her every week.

I eventually told her the truth, but it wasn't until everything fell apart.

HAPPY HOLIDAYS!! YEAH RIGHT!!

The holiday season was upon us. I was not excited about it at all. I used to love Christmas. I would decorate my house. I would go all out for my kids. I wanted them to have Christmases they would forget. I wanted them to have wonderful memories, not like the one's I had.

I used to cook for my whole family at Thanksgiving. Now that my kids have gotten older and had partners it makes it hard to get together on Thanksgiving.

I was really sad this year because I wasn't going to be having dinner with any of my family. Bennett was locked up. We couldn't be with Ali and the kids because of Blane's charges. Harmony hated Blane and didn't want to be anywhere near him. James was spending it with his girlfriend's family.

I wasn't going to cook. Then I decided that I wanted to take dinner to a woman I love and her husband. I then found out that Blane's son was going to come down from Wyoming.

I cooked two turkeys. I made all the things I usually made. The three of us sat down at the dinner table and celebrated Thanksgiving together like we were a family. As I sat there eating all I could think about was my family. I missed them. I wish I were with them; that we could have holidays be like they used to be.

Blane, went with me to deliver dinner at Ann and Ted's. He was in a big hurry to get back home. I felt so rushed. It really took the joy out of what I was doing. But what's new. He had taken my joy away a long time ago. I was now just existing. I was just going through the motions every day. I didn't care about anything. I began thinking about ending it again.

One Saturday afternoon he pulled into a home depot. We went over by the potted Christmas trees. He said, "We will get a tree like this for Christmas in a couple of weeks."

I was excited about having a tree. I hadn't decorated for the holidays in several years. He never made good on getting a tree. I wasn't going to buy it. He had been milking the shit out of me. I wasn't putting anything else out.

On Christmas Eve, he wanted me to open a gift. I did and started laughing.

He said, "What."

I said, "When we went shopping I put these sweats in the cart. I have been looking for them everywhere. You didn't pick these out for me. I picked them myself."

He thought it was funny as well.

While we took turns opening our gifts, his mother called. He took several pictures while I opened my presents. He sent them to his mom. I had to argue with him to let me take a picture of him opening his. He finally let me.

That afternoon I went to see Bennett in his program. He had screwed up and lost the pass he was going to have. They did let me take him the next day.

On New Year's Eve Blane's Uncle Willy called and asked us if we would like to go to dinner with him and his family. I told Blane that we shouldn't go. He needed to get it approved by his parole agent. He said they wouldn't do anything if they find out.

It was Blane, me, uncle Willy, his wife, their ten your old daughter, Willy's mother, and Mindy. Mindy should have put a stop to it. She knew it was a violation for him to be going out to dinner with the little girl in attendance. She thought that the rules and guidelines that he had to follow were bullshit. She just ignored them.

We all had drinks. I had two, and that was all it took. I was pretty buzzed. When we got home, we all went to the garage to smoke. I wasn't feeling all that great, so I went into bed.

The next morning Blane got up early. He came to the side of the bed and said his Dad had called and wanted him to go to breakfast with him. I said, "Okay. Have a good time," and rolled over.

A week later we went to breakfast with his Dad. I asked him if the restaurant had been busy on New Year's Day. He said, "I don't know. I didn't go anywhere that day."

I had a gut feeling for a while that Blane was up to know good. I had found makeup in my car. A ring was sitting on the coffee table. The funny thing is. I didn't care.

I was so glad when the holidays were over.

AGAINST THE WALL

Dave's rental house that was two doors down from us became vacant. He had me go down and look at it to give him a bid for cleaning. The place was trashed. I gave him my bid, but he wasn't happy with it because he was a tight wad. He always wanted to pay as little as possible. I wasn't going to budge. It was going to be a lot of scrubbing. Instead, he had his son Dale do it. He lived in Roosevelt. When he came down to do the work he stayed with us.

It was a Sunday Blane was being very distant. He left the house without telling me he was leaving. I called him multiple times. He wouldn't answer his phone. He finally called me and said, "Therapy has been canceled for tonight."

I texted his therapist to find out what was going on. He told me that Blane had called him. Blane told him that his Dad was sick and that he needed to be with him. Liar.

I continued to try and reach him. His brother asked me where he was and I told him I had no clue.

I finally left him a message and said, "Why don't you just stay with her tonight. I would enjoy having the bed all to myself." I got into bed.

A short time later he came home. He climbed into the bed. He scooted all the way over to where I was. I moved over. Then he moved over. I moved over again. He then moved over pushed up against me really hard. I fell out of the bed onto the hardwood floor. I got up off the floor and walked over to the other side of the bed. I got back in the bed. He then rolled over up against me. I scooted over. He rolled over towards me again. I fell off the bed. I jumped on top of him. I started bouncing on him. I started yelling, "You want to act like a child. Well then I can to."

He reached up and hit me. Then he took his arm and as hard as he could, he pushed me. I flew off of him, hit the wall and landed on his massage machine that was lying on the floor. I picked myself up. I stood at the foot of the bed and started yelling at him.

I said, "All you do is pick on people that are littler than you. Like those little girls. You are such a big man. You're a piece of shit." He didn't say anything. That's how he was. Just act like no big deal. Shut down and say nothing. That really pisses me off.

I walked back over and got in the bed. I was not going to let him win. I was done being pushed around by him. He scooted up against me again. I didn't move. I kept my spot.

He kept applying his weight against me. I was thinking. Fuck you, asshole. I'm not budging. Do what you want. I don't care, and I feel asleep for a few minutes.

I went to get up. I could barely move. My body hurt so bad. I started to cry because the pain was excruciating. He scooted all the way over to his side of the bed. I got up and went into the living room.

His brother was already up. I'm sure he could hear everything. He was in the room right next to us. I was really embarrassed. He didn't say anything about it. He acted like nothing was amiss.

Blane got up. We didn't speak to each other. I left for work.

I went to pick up Sheryl for work. When I walked into her house, she took one look at me and said, "What did he do?" I told her everything that had happened. She was pissed. Once again, she told me I needed to leave him. That I deserved better. I told her she was right. Just give me a minute. I'm getting things figured out.

As usual, we didn't resolve this. It got pushed under the carpet. We went to see his therapist that next Sunday. Blane told him about the incident but made it look like it was really nothing. He didn't mean to hit me. Yeah right. Just like he didn't mean for me to fall off the bed. His therapist didn't take it very seriously.

Of course, why would he? Blane was his buddy.

SHERYL DROPPED THE BOMB

I used to buy a lot of gifts for my kids and grandkids for Christmas, but I stopped doing that. Now I take them out to dinner, movie and have them choose between an outfit, toy or whatever it is they want.

It was Sunday in January. Blane had therapy. His therapist told him that he wanted just to see him; not to bring me. It happened on occasion, so I thought nothing of it. I decided to take my youngest granddaughter on her Christmas date.

We were at the Golden Corral having dinner when my phone rang. I looked at it. It was Blane's therapist. I thought hmmm wonder what he wants. Blane is supposed to be with him right now. I answered it.

He said, "Julee your friend Sheryl went to see Blane's Parole officer. She told him that you had told her that Blane had raped you." I froze. I didn't know what to say.

He said, "Julee are you there."

I said, "Oh yeah sorry my granddaughter left her seat, and I was looking around for her." That was a lie she was sitting right in front of my face. I was in shock. He continued to ask me if there was any validity to it. I said, "No." What was I supposed to say? Blane was sitting right there. I lived with him.

My mind was going a million miles a minute. What am I going to do? His therapist told me to have no contact with Sheryl. Don't call her and don't let her know that I know she went to see Larry. I said, "Ok."

I dropped my granddaughter off at home. The first thing I did was call Sheryl.

I said, "Sheryl what have you done."

Sheryl said, "What are you talking about?"

I said, "You called Larry Blane's Parole officer."

Sheryl said, "No I didn't."

I said, "His therapist just called me. He told me, you told Larry that Blane had raped me."

Sheryl said, "Julee I did. I love you. I have been watching you slip away for months. I see your pain. I feel your pain. I'm not sorry I did it. You mean so much to me that I had to do this. I can't stand watching you cry because he keeps hurting you. I love you, Julee."

I said, "I love you too. I'm not mad. What I am though is scared as shit to go home."

Sheryl said, "Do you want to come here?"

I said, "No. I have to go home. I just don't know what I'm going to say."

Sheryl said, "You have your key if you need to come over."

I said, "Okay. Don't call me or text me. The therapist said for me to not have any contact with you. I will call you and let you know what's going on. I love you, Sheryl."

Sheryl said, "I love you too. I'm here if you need me. Talk to you later."

I didn't know what to expect when I got home. I went to pull up in the driveway, Mindy's car was there. I thought oh shit. What am I going to do? She'll see right through me. I was terrified. My heart was pounding out of my chest. I could feel myself sweating. I had to go in. If I didn't come home, I would look guilty.

I went in the house. They were sitting in the family room. I went over and sat on the couch.

Blane said, "What the fuck. Why would she say something like that?"

I said, "I don't know. She is always causing drama for people. Like the roommates, she had that she made false allegations against. She doesn't want us together?" I said whatever I could think of.

Mindy said, "I think it's bullshit. There is more to it than that. Blane, you need to read between the lines.

He didn't catch that. We all went out to the garage to smoke.

I said, "I'm tired. I'm going to bed."

I went into the bedroom, put on some pajamas. I climbed onto the bed. I turned on the TV. Even though I knew I wouldn't get to watch what I wanted once he came in. He always put on what he wanted. When I would ask to watch something, he would tell me to watch it in the other room. He was always in control of things.

He came in a short time later. He was very distant. I asked him what the deal was. Has Mindy filled your head with bull shit?

He said, "The things she said make sense."

I said, "Like what?"

He said, "Don't worry about it." He climbed into the bed and said, "I'm going to sleep" and rolled on his side.

I laid there awake for what seemed like forever. I finally feel asleep in the wee hours of the morning.

Blane got up and left for work without telling me goodbye. I was relieved that he did. I didn't know what to say to him.

He called me a short time later to tell me that we needed to see his parole officer. I didn't want to go, but he said I needed to.

Once we were sitting in Larry's office, he started to talk to Blane about the internet he had installed into the house. He told him he was not allowed to have it. They went back and forth Blane saying he thought he could because they gave him permission to have it on his phone. Larry said that was only for work and nothing else. Larry went and got his supervisor.

Larry asked Blane about the allegations Sheryl had made. He also said that Sheryl's husband had called that day and said that Blane and his brother had called and threatened her life.

Shit. I knew things were over right then. Neither Blane or his brother were that stupid. Sheryl had told her husband about the time his brother threatened me. He obviously didn't listen to her. He told the probation officer wrong information.

I kept trying to get eye contact with Larry and his supervisor. Neither one of them looked at me the whole time we were there. They didn't ask me anything either. I was prepared to tell them everything.

They told Blane he had to do a lie detector test. I thought cool that will solve everything. It seemed like the day would never come for him to take it.

He took the test. He passed it. How the hell did he pass it?

I should of know he would be able to. He took one once before when we were hiding our relationship. He was doing a lot of things that he was not supposed to. He had passed that one as well. He told me himself that they are bullshit that he had passed others.

Things changed after this incident. When I would tell him no, I didn't want to have sex, he would just let it go. Sometimes he would say, "I'm not going to push it. You will tell Sheryl. Or scream rape. He would ask me every couple day's if I talked to Sheryl. I would tell him no, even though I had. I did go a couple of weeks without talking to her. That was because I didn't want to get caught. I didn't want to fight with him.

I was trying to figure out what to do.

ADULT PROBATION AND PAROLE

AP&P is nothing but a babysitting service that doesn't do a damn thing to protect the public from the felons they are paid to watch. They hardly ever came out to see Blane. When they did, they would just walk through the house. Ask a question or two and then leave. They didn't look around the property over at the apartment above the shop. When they came to the house, they didn't look in the garage or out back where the dog runs, and storage room is located.

They would slap his hand whenever he did something. Like the internet thing. I went with him to almost all of his appointments. He would sit and lie to his parole officer. He would say, "I'm being a good boy."

I hated it when he would say that. It made him look and sound like a little boy. It embarrassed me because he looked like an idiot and I was with him.

have had some roommates who were on parole. One of my roommates lived here for over a year. His parole officer came by once. My roommate was in the front yard. His parole officer stopped. Didn't even get out of his car. Chatted with my roomie then left. He never even came in to see his living environment.

I just think people need to know that they don't supervise people.

My son had several probation officers. Not one of them has ever come to my house. They constantly changed. I would call them. I could never seem to get them on the phone. It took them days to call me back.

Bennett's current probation officer is the only one who has done her job. I can call her anytime. If she doesn't answer, she calls me back within a couple of hours. She has gone out of her way to help Bennett.

Right now, as I'm writing this Bennett is on the run again. She calls me and texts me to see if I have heard anything or seen him.

THE FATAL FALL

It was now February. We got a call from Blane's stepmother. Dave fell outside of the house and broke a few ribs. He had been taken to the VA hospital. They wanted to keep him overnight. He was in a lot of pain. He had a few pain pills in his wallet. He took them without the hospital's knowledge. Along with what they were giving him and what he took it was too much for his body to handle.

He overdosed and died.

They managed to revive him. Dave already had a lot of health issues. His kidneys had been failing for quite a while. His port that they put in hadn't completely healed.

The whole family gathered at the hospital. It was touch and go for three days.

On the second day, Blane got into a car accident hurrying to the hospital. They had called him at work and told him things weren't looking good. His sister called me and told me Blane had been in a wreck. I got the information. I called and canceled my job for the day.

I hurried to the hospital to be by Blane's side. I wasn't given any information on his injuries. I walked into his room. They still had a neck brace on him. I walked over to him; his eyes were closed. I put my hand on his arm. He opened his eyes and smiled. I asked him if he was okay? What happened?

He told me the guy hit him. It wasn't his fault. He told me that they were waiting for the results from the scan. Then the nurse came in and took off the neck brace.

Then an officer came in. He gave me Blane's driver's license and proof of insurance. A copy of the accident report and the other driver's information. I told him, thank you. He said, "I hope your day gets better. I said, "Me too."

After Blane got discharged, we went straight up to the hospital. There was a lot of families there. We went into see, Dave. He didn't look good at all. His eyes were closed. I thought that he was asleep.

I said, "Blane we should say a prayer for your Dad."

Blane said a prayer and when he was done and said Amen, Dave said, "Amen."

It startled me; I didn't expect that. I held his hand. I told him I hoped that he would get better quick. I told him I loved him before I left. I'm so glad that I did because that was the last time I would see him alive.

We went to dinner that night with Blane's sister, who came from Arizona. We went to Olive Garden. She shocked me when we were in the bathroom. She told me I should dump Blane. He is a loser. You can do so much better. He will do nothing but bring you down. Wow, she just came right out and said that about her own brother. They weren't even fighting. She just feels that way.

We spent the whole next day at the hospital. His sister was trying to control everything. That's what she has always done. All Blane's kids were there. Several of Dave's kids were there. There was a lot of other people there as well.

We ordered in lunch. Nobody was going to be leaving. Dave was going downhill fast. They had decided to move him to a room where family could be in there. Half of us were down waiting in that room when we heard things had changed.

We hurried back to the waiting area where he was. I walked over to the door leading to the ICU. Blane came bursting out. He was sobbing. He grabbed hold of me. I wrapped my arms tightly around him. He held me so tight.

He said, "I love you so much. I need you."

He sobbed for a long time. We went over into the waiting room. Everyone was crying. He got on his knees in front of his two daughters who were sitting in chairs and hugged them.

He was sitting next to me when his little niece, who is maybe ten, stopped in front of him. He reached out and pulled her to him. He hugged her. I felt like he was hugging her way to long. I looked over at his daughter. She was watching him too. Nothing was ever said.

After Dave had passed things got crazy. Blane's family started searching for a will. Everybody wanted his stuff, and he had a lot. His illegitimate kids started coming out of the woodwork. His family is a mess. He has a brother that is so close in age it's ridiculous. His mother and his brother's mother met in the doctor's waiting room. Both pregnant with Dave's children Blane and Louis. That must have been quite a shock for both of them.

It turns out the Uncle Willy and Aunt Annie were really his older brother and sister. Then there was Spice who came on the seen a few years ago; another of his illegitimate children. Then there was one that had died. Dave had made a lot of children, and they all wanted their share.

I had been asking Blane to finish Bennett's room for me for the last few months. He kept putting it off. Bennett was going to be getting out. I needed his room done so he could come home. Now I didn't know what I was going to do.

Blane got his brother to come to my house and help him finish it. Blane put one of the windows in the wrong way. I know his mind was somewhere else. He had just lost his Dad, and it was in the morning.

I didn't get upset about it. I am upset about the other work he did in my house when he wasn't distracted. He did a shitty job. His craftsmanship was horrible, and if I were him, I would be ashamed of it. The work that Mindy did looked great.

The day of the memorial service his son came to the house. The three of us rode to the service together. I was going to be the designated driver. The place that they had the service was beautiful. They had servers walking around with hors d'oevres, and drinks. Blane took a bottle of crown. His son took Yager.

There was a lot of people at his services. We weren't there very long when I found myself alone. I went looking for Blane. I found him; he had his arm draped over some woman's shoulder.

He then walked around with her for quite a long time. Stopping to talk to different people. I walked up to them. He just glanced at me.

I felt like I didn't belong there. I went outside and sat by the gas light fireplace. I sat there for about an hour. I began to cry. It was my Daddy's birthday. He hadn't even been gone a year. I had mentioned it to Blane earlier that day. It was like he didn't even care. My feelings didn't matter. I felt so lost and alone. My heart was breaking. I was sad that Dave was dead. I was missing my Dad. I wanted to just get up and leave. Let him find his own way home. I couldn't bring myself to do it. I know that he needed me. I needed to be there for him.

While I was sitting at the fire, Mindy came over. Her kids came over as well. She was drunk. She was also supposed to be watching Blane. As his sponsor, she was supposed to watch him. There were a lot of children running around. He was to be watched at all times.

When we got home, I sat on the couch for a few minutes. I told Blane I was tired and was going to bed. He stayed up to hang out with his son. I was crying when he came to bed.

He said, "What are you boobing about?" In a nasty cold-hearted tone.

I said nothing. I rolled onto my side and went to sleep. Why should I tell him? I already did that day. Obviously, he wasn't listening; which seemed to be the case most of the time. It got to where I wouldn't tell him anything.

The next day they had the service at the cemetery. I sat by myself while Blane sat with his siblings. I drove there by myself because Bennett was home. It really sucked because the speaker wasn't working. The bugle that was supposed to play taps didn't work either. Other than that, it was a nice service.

When I left, I walked over to where Joe was buried. I stood there for several minutes. I don't know about anyone else, but I talk to those who have passed on as if there still right there with me. I proceeded to tell him how much I missed him. I told him what a mess I had made of my life. How I wished he was still here.

Blane's brother, from out of state, came to town a few days later. He was obviously wanting to make sure he was going to get his slice of the pie. He stayed at our house for several days.

Bennett had been released from his program. He was back home. I was going to be staying at my house. Blane had asked me several times to talk to his Dad about him living with us. I was not about to have my son live with him. I was not going to subject him to his cruelty. I could only imagine what kind of hell he would put my boy through. I sure didn't want to find out either. I never asked my ex.

I went to the house the evening of the cemetery service. Blane got pissed he said, "You should be home with Bennett. He just got out."

I said, "I know. I just wanted to make sure you were okay."

I don't think he wanted me there. I only stayed for a few minutes and then I left.

GIRLS GONE WILD

Sapphire had invited Harmony and me to a party at her house. It was a girl's party with adult novelties. I didn't tell Blane about it; he would have told me I couldn't go or would have made me feel guilty if I did. Lose, Lose situation.

While I was at the party, he called me. I didn't want to answer it, but I knew if I didn't he would accuse me of being with someone else. So, I answered it. I decided to tell him where I was. I told him about the party. What did he do? He started making me feel guilty. He said, "You should be home with Bennett. You need to figure out your priorities."

After I got off the phone with him, I just sat there. The wind had been let out of my sail. I just wanted to go home.

I went to the house the next day. He wouldn't talk to me. I tried talking to him, but he just kept ignoring me. I started crying.

I told him I went to the party to see if they had anything that would help us enjoy each other more. That was a lie. I went because I wanted to be around friends, and have a good time for a change. It had nothing do to with the adult toys. I just wanted to have some fun, and I did until he called.

Bennett took off again. This time he was only gone for a couple of weeks before he decided to come back home.

LOCKED OUT

I had decided that I want to surprise Blane by showing up to our counseling session with my hair done and makeup on. My roommate's girlfriend was doing my hair.

While I was getting ready, he called me. He told me he did not want me to come to the appointment. I asked why. He told me he didn't want me there.

It was kind of odd when he called.

Mindy had arrived at my house shortly before he called. I think that they had it planned. He probably wanted to see how I was going to react. I got very upset. I said, "Why is he doing this to me? Why has he been so ignorant to me?"

His daughter happened to call me during all of this. I told her you don't know the things your Dad has done to me. I couldn't stop crying. She said everything would be okay. If she knew the things, he does she would have never thought that.

I called him later when I knew he was out of counseling. He told me he was changing the locks. In other words, that was not my home anymore. I told him he could not do that. It is just as much my house as his.

He said, "Watch me."

We texted a whole bunch of ugly stuff to each other. I finally turned my phone off.

The next day Harmony and I drove over to the house. He had changed the locks. I was pissed. I was done. I didn't care what happened to him at this point. I immediately called his parole officer. I asked him if I could see him. He said, "Yes."

Harmony and I drove straight to his office. I told him that everything Sheryl had told him was true. I explained how her husband got things wrong when it came to the threats. I told him about the time Blane had hit Bennett. I told him about all the things he had done in the halfway house that he wasn't supposed to do. I told him about the dinner with the minor child. I spilled everything. Except all of the other abuse because I was still ashamed that I had let it happen for as long as I had.

Larry said, "There was nothing we could do about him hitting Bennett because it was in his last parole and he had already gone back to prison. That made absolutely no sense to me. It was a crime. He had never been charged so just because he went back to jail for something else he doesn't have to pay a consequence for that. I think its bull shit.

Larry said, "He passed the lie detector test so there is nothing I can do."

I asked him if I could take one. He said, "We wouldn't want to put you through something like that."

I said, "I don't care. I will do it."

He wouldn't let me. I asked what I could do about the rape in September.

He said, "If I wanted I could file a police report and see what they would do.

I said, "Okay, I will."

Larry asked me why I hadn't said something when I was in his office with Blane.

I told him that I kept trying to make eye contact. I said, "Did you ever look at me, Larry?"

He thought for a second and then said, "No I didn't."

I continued to tell him that I also kept trying to get eye contact with his supervisor and he never looked at me either. I got the feeling that he felt bad about what happened that day. He didn't say it, but I could feel it.

We left his office, and I decided that I was going to go get a protective order. I was afraid that once he found out, I had gone to see Larry he might do something crazy. I also wanted him out of that house. It wasn't right for him to take sole possession.

I went to the court house. I was there most of the day. They granted me a temporary protective order. He was to leave the house. He was also ordered to stay away from my home in Glendale.

I called the police and made a report for the time he raped me in September. They told me that a detective would be calling me.

I called the West Valley police and told them that I had a protective order that I need them to help me serve. They told me to call them when I got over by the house. I parked down the street by his Dad's rental house while I waited for them to arrive.

After they had got them I drove down to the house. I sat in my van while they were in the house with him. They served him with the protective order.

I was sitting in my car across the street when he came flying out of the driveway in his truck. He drove it to his Dad's rental house two doors down. He walked back to the house to get his little sports car. He glared at me; I smile at him. He locked the house up tight so I couldn't get in.

The police told me that they could not make him give them or me the keys. I had to call a locksmith. I don't know much about them. I got screwed hard. I ended up paying 800 dollars to get into the house.

While I was standing on the front porch with the locksmith guys, Mindy and Blane drove by. One of them yelled out of her truck that I better watch my back. The guy standing next to me asked if I was going to be alright.

I said, "I'll be fine." In reality, I was scared shitless. I have heard of some of the things the two of them had done in their past. I could only imagine what they were going to do to me.

That night I didn't sleep a wink. I jumped at every noise. The next morning, I went to work as usual. It was exhausting. Thank God, I had Sheryl not only did she do her work but ended up doing half of mine. It was also wonderful to have her moral support. She assured me that this too shall pass. I would be Okay.

At 5:00 PM I drove into the parking lot of Bennett's old school. I was going there because they had free lawyer's advice. I saw a car with this lady in it that looked familiar. All of a sudden, a bunch of teenagers came running towards my car. It was Bennett and his friends. He had decided to turn himself in. He wanted to get things taken care of and come home.

I told him what was going on. He sat with me while I was talking to the law student about my situation. They weren't much help.

We went to the house after we left. I had taken Bennett over their a few times on his passes to see his dog. It would be his first time sleeping there.

That night as he was sleeping I began to unravel. I started thinking that it was time for me to go. I couldn't handle the stress anymore. The nightmares had gotten worse. I would wake up terrified. I just wanted it all to stop.

The next day, I called Bennett's Probation officer. She told me exactly what I already thought she would say. She told me to drop him off at the detention center. It was good because I didn't want him to watch me deteriorate. He went willingly.

We went to court a couple of days later. They said he had to stay in the detention center for a couple of weeks. Bennett was pissed. He was going to miss Easter with the family. He hadn't spent the holidays with us for a long time. It was no one's fault but his own. He chose to commit crimes, use drugs, and to run away from home when he was supposed to be working on things to stay in our home.

Blane's sister from Arizona called me. One of the neighbors had notified her that Blane was staying in the vacant rental property. She asked me what was going on. I told her. She told me I needed to get camera's put on the house. I needed to be very careful because he was dangerous. She filled me with fear. She told me I needed to tell his probation officer that he was right down the street.

She just wanted him out of the house because it was one of the family assets. I told her he had left a bunch of paperwork laying around. She had me explain to her what it was. Then she asked me to email it to her.

I got a text from Blane with a picture. She got the same one. I got very scared she told me to go to the police station. I went to a different one because I didn't want to deal with West Valley Police. His son-in-law is a police officer there.

I was there for over an hour waiting to talk to someone. He told the officers that he had sent the text and picture as multimedia and it went to all his contacts. They let it go. I accidentally called his number as well and hung up immediately. They let that go too.

I felt like I was starting to slip away. I was not eating. Hardly sleeping. I had gotten a bad cold. I was smoking cigarette after cigarette. I was getting very weak. I wasn't going to work. I couldn't. I would get light headed when I would stand. I was falling apart. I kept hearing the back-fence open. I was losing it.

Harmony was staying with me. She kept trying to get me to eat. I would eat a little just to make her happy. I didn't like seeing her worry. She took me to see my doctor. We told him what was going on. I told him I couldn't sleep. He prescribed me some sleeping pills.

I could see that things were starting to wear on Harmony. I told her I would be okay, that she could go home.

EASTER PARTY

I decided that I wanted to have my whole family get together. I bought food, and stuff for coloring eggs. Everyone came and brought their kids and more food.

I was standing in the house looking at everyone outside on the camera monitor when my nephew walked up and put his arm around me.

He said, "Julee, you need to go outside and be with your family. Not watch them through the screen."

He was right. I needed to stop being on the outside; I needed to be a part of the family. I went outside and watched the kids color eggs.

My son James told me that he had driven past Blane as he was driving to the house.

He said, "I waved at him, but he didn't wave back."

I told him that he was not allowed to have any kind of contact with my family or me.

It turned out to be a great day. Ali, her boyfriend and I stood out by her jeep because they wanted to have a beer. I had told everyone that I didn't want any alcohol at the party.

Bennett called while we were coloring eggs. He was upset that his probation officer had decided to make him stay in detention until the day after Easter. I was upset about it too. I haven't had all four of my children together in one place since the day I married Joe.

I was really happy that I was able to have everyone over. I had court on the 30th for the protective order. I didn't know what was going to happen. I wanted to have at least one great memory of my family at that house.

My two youngest granddaughters asked if they could spend the night. I wasn't sure if it would be a good thing at first. I then thought about it. It would be nice, to spend some time with the girls. I hadn't done Easter with them for quite a long time.

The next morning Harmony came over early. I told the girls that we needed to go to the store so I could get smokes. We went to the store. I told them they could get what they wanted. I called Harmony.

She wasn't done hiding the eggs. I told the girls I needed to go back to the store that I needed a lighter. We went to a different store. I was trying to waste time so that Harmony could finish hiding the eggs; we had colored a lot of them.

Once we got back to the house, I got all excited. I told the girls that I thought I had heard the Easter bunny last night. I said, "I think we need to see if he hid any eggs."

They both got really excited. I gave them each a bag; the hunt was on.

They were searching for the eggs for a long time. It seems like every Easter there are a couple of eggs that can't be found. We all had to start searching.

Harmony couldn't remember where she hid them all. It was great. I hadn't been on an Easter egg hunt in years. I was actually hunting for eggs.

I took the girls home after that. I visited at Ali's for a very short time. I was starting to feel exhausted again. I had lost several pounds by this time due to everything that was going on.

On that Monday, I went to pick up Bennett from the detention center. I had made him an Easter basket full of candy. He dug right into it. We spent that day, just watching TV.

Bennett fell asleep on the couch. I went into the bedroom to lay down.

I had been struggling with my thoughts all day. I didn't want to be here anymore. I felt like my life had no meaning. I wasn't any good to anybody. I was terrified of going to court. I didn't want to face Blane. I knew he would bring a bunch of his family and Mindy. I didn't see my life getting any better. I felt like my business was falling apart and to be honest I didn't care. I'm tired of cleaning everyone's house. I thought of all the reasons why I should just end it once and for all.

I began praying. I told God I was coming home. I told him I couldn't live with the pain anymore. Then I heard it clear as day.

"You have a purpose."

I cried out what. What is my purpose? I started bawling; I had to do something. I needed someone to be there with me. I was so afraid that I was losing my mind.

I didn't want to wake Bennett. I hated the fact that he had already seen how messed up I was. I got on my phone. I went to Facebook. I saw that my niece was online. I messaged her that I needed help.

She called me immediately. I told her that I was having horrible thoughts; that I wasn't doing very good. She is very familiar with our family's mental health issues. She knew what was happening to me. I was having a nervous breakdown. I had been going downhill the last couple of weeks. It was getting worse. I knew that I had to reach out.

She told me she would try to find a ride over. She called me back to let me know that no one would give her a ride. I told her to take a cab. I would pay for it when she got there. When she showed up, she had her boyfriend with her. I was not happy about that. I didn't know him. I didn't say anything to her.

We went into the bedroom to talk. We both sat up on the bed. I began telling her what was going on. I could see the love and concern in her eyes. She hugged me real tight.

She said, "I love you Aunt Julee. I got your back." She told me I should lay down and get some rest.

The next morning, she asked me what I wanted to eat. I told her one scrambled egg. That's all I had been able to eat for the last couple weeks. Anything else made my stomach hurt.

I had been making videos of myself. I was posting them on Facebook. I was talking about a lot of stuff. My family was becoming very concerned about my well-being.

I was having a mental breakdown. Some of the stuff was out there. But some of the things I talked about weren't. Like God. I talked about his saving grace how he was with me. Well, he was and still is.

I talked about demons in these videos. How they were out to get me. I believed that because I have encountered so many evil people in my life. The videos are still out there. One popped up on my Facebook as a memory posted. Feel free to locate them if you want. You will see what was taking place at that time.

Patricia and her boyfriend drove me around town to take care of things that had to be done before I went to court on the protective order. I was trying to get things organized and put in place.

I think about it now, and I don't think I did.

COURT

I tossed and turned all night, I was terrified, I had court today. I hadn't talked to or seen Blane in two weeks. I got up to get in the shower. I tried to wake Patricia up. She wouldn't wake up at first. I began getting very anxious and frustrated.

I yelled at her, "Get the fuck up!"

I had had terrible mood swings. I would go from crying hysterically, then anger, fear, sadness and hopelessness.

Patricia wanted me to eat something. I told her no, I can't. She told me I needed to, that it would help me feel better. Nothing at this point was going to make me feel better.

We took Bennett to school on the way to court. I gave him a big hug. I told him how much I loved him; that I would be there to pick him up after school. He told me he hoped everything would go okay in court.

He said, "I love you, mama."

My heart melts every time one of my children calls me mama. When I hear that it reminds me that I have done something great in my life, I have brought four beautiful human beings into this world.

We got to the courthouse; we were early. Blane was sitting on the bench in the hallway. Mindy and Willy are the only ones I remember being there. He may have had others with him, but I don't recall.

Harmony met us at the courthouse. I was shaking uncontrollably; I was terrified. Patricia was trying to keep me calm. She walked me to the bathroom where she gave me a pep talk. My nephew was supposed to come but hadn't arrived.

Finally, it was time to go in. Just as we were heading in my nephew showed up. I didn't have a chance to talk to him. I hadn't seen him since Easter. He knew that I was struggling from the videos. Patricia was also keeping my sister posted on what was going on with me.

I sat down in the seats where you wait for your turn to see the Judge. I watched as she saw some other cases. She was very direct. She was very callous. I began to get scared. I wanted just to get up and run; I knew I couldn't.

It was my turn. The Bailiff showed me were to sit. He didn't need to. I had been to court some many times in my life that I knew where to go. I sat down in my chair.

I don't remember what the Judge was saying. She gave me the opportunity to talk. She kept interrupting me. I began to anger and frustrated.

My nephew stood up and ask if he could speak on my behalf.

I turned around and in a mean, angry, nasty tone, told him, "I could do this myself. I don't need your help." I turned back around.

The Judge said, "Are you afraid of Blane?"

At that moment, I was angry; I was not afraid of anything, which is part of my psychotic breakdown. My feelings change in a flash. When in reality I was afraid. She then hit her gavel and said case dismissed. I tried to say something, and she ordered me out of her courtroom.

I started yelling. It was crazy. My family ushered me to the elevator. I was going off. The bailiff followed us to the elevator. I didn't know where Harmony was. I told my sister to find her. She was having a meltdown as well. She made a comment about killing herself.

They detained her for a few minutes before they would let her leave.

THROWN OUT OF THE HOUSE

We headed straight to the house. I knew Blane was going to go straight there to take back possession. When we got there, he was there along with Mindy and Willy.

The police were called. It was going to get ugly. He stood out by the street with his little clan. I was talking with the police in the driveway. While I was doing that Patricia and her boyfriend were getting their stuff loaded in the truck, they were also getting some of my stuff. I didn't know it at the time, but they were also helping themselves to some of our things. They stole my 13-inch TV, Bose stereo that Joe had given me, and all my jewelry.

When I was done talking with the officers, I went into the house. Blane had also come in. Mindy came in as well. I told her to get out.

She said, "Make me."

I yelled at her, "Get the fuck out of my house!" I said, "I'm not afraid of you. You want to fight bitch. Let's do it."

Blane heard what was going on. He came over and said, Mindy, come on. We don't need any more problems with the police. They both went out the back door and stood in the driveway. We got everything loaded that I was taking with me at that time, then we left. I had to leave my big dogs because I didn't have room for them in the van.

    stood up to Mindy that day. Several days before that I was loading stuff to take to my house. I couldn't find my Dad's knives. I thought Blane had stolen them.

    I called my step-sister crying. I told her about the knives. She came right over. We called the police. While we were waiting for them, we sat on the front porch. Mindy had driven past. I told my sister who she was. I hurried into the house. I said, "Sis you see her down there.?"

    She said, "Yes."

I told her that I was terrified of her. I didn't want to come out of the house. She could see my fear. She didn't understand. I used to not be afraid like that. So, that day I stood up to her it was awesome. I was back or was I just in my psychotic state and feeling invincible.

I did eventually find my knives, for which I was grateful. They aren't worth a lot of money. They were sentimental. I left all my furniture along with other things. I didn't know what he would do with my stuff, but I was hoping he would not be vindictive and destroy it or sell it.

We went back to my house. Patricia's boyfriend drove the truck, and she drove my van. I wish I had taken the time to look in the back of my truck. I would have seen all the things they had stolen. They were saying that they had got kicked out of their place. They needed to take my truck to their house to get their things and then find a new place to stay. I let them take my truck.

Big mistake.

I picked Bennett up from school. We went back to our house.

James called and said he was coming over. He wanted to talk to me. I knew what he wanted. He wanted to take me to the hospital.

I told Bennett we have to go.

LOCKED IN

I hurried and grabbed a few things. We had to get out of their quick. I knew James was going to make me go to the hospital. I didn't want to be locked up.

Bennett and I went down to North Temple where we rented a room at the hotel. After we had got our room, we went to get something to eat. The toilet in our room was broken. I went to the office and requested a different room. They were very apologetic about the broken toilet and gave us another room.

I told Bennett we should go to California. I talked to his probation officer about it. She said I couldn't take Bennett anywhere. That squashed that idea.

Bennett fell asleep watching TV. I couldn't sleep, my mind was going a mile a minute. I didn't know what was happening. I was so confused.

It was early in the morning. I hadn't slept at all. I went in to use the bathroom. I went to open the door to come out. It wouldn't open. I kept trying to open it. She had locked me in. I began screaming and pleading with my mother to let me out. I began banging my head against the wall.

"Mom please let me out. I will be good. Please let me out."

I was sitting on the floor with my back against the wall. I had my legs pulled up to my chest and my arms wrapped around my legs and my head down. I began to cry quietly. I then stood up and tried the door again. It opened up.

Bennett never woke up. I walked over to him and tried to wake him up. We needed to leave. I was in a panic. I had to go.

I tried to call James. My phone would not cooperate. I took a picture of Bennett and posted it on Facebook with the address of where we were.

I said, "Somebody, please come save my boy." Something like that I can't remember for sure what it said.

I gathered my things. I kissed Bennett on the forehead then I left. I didn't take my van because I didn't feel safe driving. I didn't want to hurt anyone. I headed up North Temple towards downtown. I was waiting for the Trax train when James called me. He told me he was at the hotel with Bennett. He asked me to come back. He wanted to talk to me.

I said, "Okay."

James, Kennedy, Bennett and a Salt Lake City police officer were standing in the hotel parking lot. I walked up to them.

The police officer asked, "Are you, Julee?"

I said, "Yes sir. I am."

The police officer said, "We received a call about yelling and screaming that was coming from your room."

I said, "That was me. I'm having some issues."

The police officer said, "Your family is very concerned."

I said, "I know. I'm going to let them take me to the hospital to get checked out. I want to get a drug test done, to prove that my behavior is not drug related. I have had a lot of things going on that has caused me great distress."

The police officer said, "I'm going to let you go. You need to go with your son straight to the hospital."

I said, "Okay but first we have to drop Bennett off at school."

The police officer said, "That's fine." Then he headed back to his car.

We all rode in James's car to the hospital. We went to Intermountain. When we got there, they took me right back to a room. James and Kennedy went back with me. A short time later Harmony showed up.

I was in the room for just a few minutes when a nurse came in. She asked me some questions. She came back with a hospital gown for me to put on. She said they needed to do an exam. I didn't think anything of it. So, I changed. A few minutes later the doctor came in and started asking me questions.

She wanted to know if I was suicidal. I proceeded to tell her that I was not suicidal. I proceeded to tell her about my last visit there in October of 2013. I guess I told her a bunch of other things as well.

I told her I'm not homicidal or suicidal so you can't keep me. She left the room. A person appeared with a desk and a chair and set outside my door. I said, "I need to go to the bathroom." That person got up and followed me there and back. I knew what was up. They were going to lock me up. I got on my phone. I posted a video of Facebook asking for my friends to help me. I said a lot of stuff on that video. I tried to contact a lawyer but was unable to get that done it time.

My phone rang. It was a detective that was assigned to the rape charge that I had reported a couple of days prior. He said he was going on vacation and would be gone for a couple of weeks. We made an appointment for me to see him in his office in two weeks.

I got up off the bed I was going to bolt. Suddenly standing in the doorway were several officers and others.

All of a sudden, I went back to that hot August summer night. I backed up. I grabbed anything I could get my hands on and started throwing it at them.

James, Kennedy, and Harmony left the room. They were coming towards me. I began swinging. They grabbed me. I was screaming that I'm not going to let you kill me like you killed Brett. I fought with everything I had.

I lost.

They carried me to a gurney in the hall put me on it and strapped me down. They immediately started rolling it to the doors. I rolled passed James and Kennedy. James looked really sad. I know it must have hurt him deeply to see his mama in that condition. I'm not sure where Harmony was, but I know that this was causing her great pain as well.

When they wheeled my out of the hospital, it was really windy. The medivac helicopter was sitting on its pad with the propellers going. It was really loud. I thought it was awesome.

They put me in the ambulance. The guy that was back there with me was absolutely gorgeous. I let him know that. I was able to sit up enough to look out the window. Everything seemed so bright. I felt exhilarated. I don't why. Probably part of the episode I was in.

They wheeled me down the hall to the locked unit at University Psychiatric Hospital. They took off the restraints and put me in a small room. It had a couch, love seat, a table in the corner with a lamp on it, and a fan.

A lady came in to talk to me. She asked if it would be okay if she asked me some questions.

I said, "Sure ask away."

She asked me all the basic stuff like my name, address, and some other things. Then she asked if I had ever hit my head.

Suddenly, I felt a steel toed boot hit the back of my head. I fell onto the floor. I put one arm across my stomach and was reaching up with the other to block the kicks that were coming straight at my stomach.

I began screaming, "Stop, Stop!"

I had gone back to an incident that happened in the 80's when I was with Brett.

There is a lot more to tell you about concerning that day. I will be putting all the details in the next book that tells the whole story of my life with Brett.

The lady hurried out of the room. I got up closed the door. I began barricading the door. I pushed the couch in front of the door and then piled everything else on it. I was not letting him in. I was standing there looking at the stuff against the door when I was grabbed from behind. I hadn't noticed that there were two doors.

I was escorted by a couple of very large gentlemen, to a room that had nothing in it but a bed. The room was dark and cold. They let me go. I moved all the way back into the corner. A different lady was standing by the door.

A few minutes later a doctor arrived. He began asking me some stuff. I told him he was very attractive.

I was blunt, with everyone. I said whatever I thought not caring about what they thought of me. Those two big guys reappeared. The doctor said he had some medicine that they needed to give me. I told him I'm not taking your drugs.

He said, "I could cooperate, or they would have to take other measures. You need to lay down on the bed."

I thought about it for a second. I could fight them, but I knew that I would lose. There was more of them, and they were much bigger than me.

I walked over to the bed and laid on my stomach. I said to one of the guys, "Can I squeeze your hand?"

He gave me his hand. They injected me in both hips.

I don't remember anything for the next week. I went to the hospital to pick up my paperwork. I wanted to see what happened while I was there. I only have a memory of a couple of visits.

remember Harmony, Sheryl, Danni, and Sapphire visiting. I was all talking about building my cleaning business. I had all kinds of ideas.

Harmony commented that we need to just work on getting me better. Harmony took care of my business while I was there. She did a great job. She cleaned the houses, made all necessary phone calls. I'm so blessed to have such a wonderful daughter. She came to see me almost every day.

I don't remember a lot of the visits. She told me I would try to convince her to get admitted so we could have some fun.

My wonderful girlfriend Kitty from church came to see me. She brought a bunch of candy. We all sat there and ate it because they said I couldn't keep it.

Blane came to see me. I don't remember it at all. I guess he brought me a bunch of makeup, markers, crayons, colored pencils, and coloring books.

thought Harmony had brought me all of those things because she had gone shopping and bought me a bunch of new clothes.

I do remember him calling me a few days before my release. He told me Angel was eating herself alive. She chews herself when she gets stressed out. He said he has never seen her do it this bad before.

I told him I would try to get ahold of my niece and have her get her.

I tried to no avail to reach her. She still had my truck and was nowhere to be found. I called him to let him know that I couldn't do anything until I got out. He said, "Whatever it's your dog."

My friend Mark came to see me. I asked him to pick up the rent from my roommates and to stop-in and check on things at the house for me.

He said, "Sure thing. Is there anything else you need?"

I told him no that was it. I don't remember anything else we talked about.

I called Ali and asked her to come see me and bring the girls.

She said, "No. I don't want the girls to see you in there. When you get out, we will come see you, or you can come to the house."

At first it made me really sad. Then after some thought, I knew she was right. I'm glad that she made that call it was the right one.

My favorite client sent me a beautiful plant. They kept it in the nurse's station where I could see it. I remember talking to her on the phone twice. She called a lot more than that, but that is all I remember.

I had made friends with a few of the other patients. There was this young girl that I became very fond of. We hung out a lot. She talked about needing a job when she got out. I told her I would give her a try. We were both Christians.

They didn't offer a Christian church service so we asked if we could call and have someone come in. They said that was fine.

A very nice women who had been ordained as a pastor came to see us. The three of us sat in a room and had talked about God and his love for us. We also talked about other things. In the end, the lady gave a beautiful prayer.

My pastor called me. He told me that God was in control. Things would work out the way they are supposed to. He said that they are praying for me.

I told him, "Thank you so much for calling. I know that I'm going to be alright. That God was with me. I feel him working on my behalf."

There was this one guy. He was quiet and kept to himself. He always had a book in his hands. I said, "You read a lot."

He said, "Yes."

I said, "I'm going to write a book. I'm going to name it Preyed Upon by A Predator."

He said, "Really, I will read it."

I said, "The author's name will be JULEEKAY. One name and that's it."

He said, "I will be watching for it."

I think a lot of people say they are going to do something when they are in a psychotic state. I may have been way out there, but I knew I had to share what has happened in order to help others that may be suffering the same things that I have endured.

One day, a staff member started talking to me. She made the comment that we had gotten close with all the time we had spent together.

I just starred at her. I only remember one interaction with her. It was that first day. She was standing in the doorway of the time out room. I remember asking her if I could leave the room right after they gave me the injection. She told me we had to wait to give the meds time to work.

There was this one male staff that was great. He took me outside. We would talk about how it would be nice for them to put flowers in certain areas of the yard. He was very kind. He had a beautiful daughter that worked there as well.

The doctor was a very handsome man, late 30's, dark curly hair. He had very kind eyes. I would stare at him when I was telling him things. I made a few inappropriate comments. I liked the way it made him smile.

He wrote in one of his reports that I stated that God had saved me. He guides my steps. I told him that I hear him speak to me. I still agree with that. He did save me, and he guides me each and every day. He is always with me. He does talk to me. He talks to everyone if you would slow done enough to listen. You need to believe that he is the Alpha and Omega. The beginning and the end.

I also talked about demons. Yes, there are demons walking this earth. Some of them come in human form. They look for weak people and then take advantage of them.

I kept saying that I wanted to leave. They wanted me to stay so they set up a court with the mental health people. They were going to try to commit me as an involuntary patient.

Harmony came up to the hospital that morning. We had a meeting with the doctor. I told him I would stay. They still had me go downstairs to the place they held their hearings. We waited in the waiting area for about an hour when one of the staff members approached us.

He said, "You don't have to go to court. You have agreed to stay so we can bypass this."

The three of us went back upstairs to the unit. Harmony stayed for a little bit. I hated to see her go. I always felt sad when she would leave.

I stayed for another week.

I know I needed to stay and get regulated on the new medication. I know that I was very sick and needed the help they were giving me. I was finally starting to feel like I was gaining control over my feelings and actions. I would go from happy, sad, angry, violent, etc. within seconds. The meds were starting to help.

The day finally came for me to leave. I waited anxiously for Harmony to get there. Once she was there, we still had to wait to see the doctor. He wanted to see me one last time before I left. He told me how important it was for me to continue therapy and to take my medication.

I assured him that I was going to do aftercare.

RAPE INTERVIEW

When they admitted me to the hospital, Bennett ran, again. He was only gone for a few days. He was stopped and arrested for being intoxicated. The state sent him to another program. They sent him down south in hopes that being far away would help.

It's amazing how things work out. I had forgotten that I had an appointment with the detective. I looked at the calendar on my phone when I got in the car to leave the hospital. My appointment was in an hour. Just enough time for us to drive there.

We checked in at the desk. The detective came out to get us and took us upstairs. He had Harmony wait in the conference room. We went down the hall to an interview room. I told him everything that had happened on that September night. I didn't tell him about all the other times. I still hadn't been able to bring myself to do that. I gave him the list of names and numbers of those I had talked to right after it happened. He told me he would do his interviews and then call me and let me know what would happen next.

Later that day I went to Blane's to get my dogs. I really needed to see Angel. Blane was right she had chewed herself raw. I went in and sat on the couch. He sat down next to me.

He said, "How are you feeling?"

I said, "Much better."

He said, "That's good. I was really worried about you."

I said, "Really?"

He said, "Yes. Did I pick out the right makeup?"

I said, "What are you talking about?"

He said, "I brought you makeup, markers, and stuff to color?"

I said, "I thought Harmony bought that when she bought me my new clothes."

He said, "You had mentioned when I first talked to you that you wanted to start wearing makeup. You also talked about how coloring made you feel better. So, I decided to bring you those things."

I said, "Thank you and gave him a hug."

I then went out to get my dogs. I was feeling really shitty. I had just reported him for the rape. I would go back and forth with myself. Yeah, he did do this nice thing for you. What about all the ugly things he's done to you. It was always a fight in my head; Love and Hate.

It felt really strange being alone in my room. I really wasn't alone; I had my dogs. I didn't have a TV hooked up, so I just laid on my bed staring at the ceiling. I didn't hook up a TV until Christmas.

Several weeks later the detective called me. He told me he had finished his investigation and was ready to turn it over to the District Attorney. I was still feeling unstable. I didn't know if I could go through this without falling apart again. I told the detective I couldn't do it; I'm scared. I still feel sick. He told me it was alright. We could hold off. The case would still be there when I was ready to move forward. I told him, "Thank you for understanding."

BYE BYE BOAT

I had asked Blane the day I went to get my dogs if he would help me get my boat ready to sell.

He asked, "What's in it for me?"

I told him I would split the profit with him.

He said, "Okay." He told me where to purchase the vinyl paint to redo the seats.

I had paid Mindy to help me the year before. When I left, she used a different cleaner on the seats. It did a great job. So, we thought. I think it must had stripped them because after being in the sun for a bit they turned an ugly orange rust color. They were hideous.

I went to his house to clean the boat. We worked together and got it all finished. It was actually a very nice evening. It had been a long time since we enjoyed time together.

When we were done with the boat, we had dinner together. He never even attempted to make a move on me. I was afraid that he was going to and I had already told myself I would not let it happen.

He took pictures of the boat. He then put it up for sale on KSL. The people would call me. Then I would call him to see if he was going to be home to show it. I'm not good at selling things, so I needed him to handle that part for me.

We had several people look at it. One guy said he wanted it but ended up having trouble getting a loan. I had a couple of guys that wanted to look at it, but Blane had plans. I went ahead and made arrangements to meet them.

Blane's mom and sister were visiting from Arizona. When Harmony and I got to the house, they were sitting outside on the patio. We walked over and said Hello. After a few minutes of small talk, Blane's mother said Harmony shouldn't be there.

I said, "Yes she can. She is 20."

She thought Harmony was still a minor.

I said, "I wouldn't bring a minor around Blane."

I heard the people walking up the driveway. I walked over and introduced myself. We all took the cover off the boat. They started looking at things. I just stepped aside and let them have at it. They asked me some questions, and I answered them to the best of my ability. They wanted the boat.

While they were looking at the boat the other guy, who wanted it texted me. He had gotten approved. He wanted to meet me at the bank in the morning. I didn't know what to do.

I went over at sat at the table on the patio. They came up to me and gave me an offer. I told them I had to have full price. They said they were going to go out front to talk.

A few minutes later I walked out there. I told them about the other guy who wanted it. I said I was going to let him have it.

They said, "We really want it. We will give you full price plus an extra thirty-five dollars if you will take our deposit tonight. We can meet you at your bank tomorrow to finalize things."

I thought for a minute. Then I agreed. We filled out a paper stating what we had agreed upon.

The next day I met one of the guys at the bank. We got everything all taken care of. He wanted to go right over to get the boat. I called Blane to ask him if I could get the garage code so that I could give this guy all the life jackets and boating toys.

He asked me what I sold it for. I told him the price that his mother and sister had heard them offer me. He said I shouldn't have done that. I should have held out for the full price. I told him I was going to give him three hundred dollars.

He got pissed off and said that's bullshit you said half. He wouldn't give me the garage code. He told me I could get them later. Then he hung up.

We went over to the house so that he could take his boat. It felt so good knowing that I know longer had to make payments. I really didn't think Blane deserved anything. I had paid to get it ready once before, and he wouldn't help me post it because he didn't want me to sell it. I made all of the payments. I paid for the maintenance. I always bought the food when we took it out. He did help pay for gas on our outings. He also did some repairs but not enough to warrant me paying him more money when I sold it. He should have been happy for me. He knew how much I stressed over the payments.

Harmony and I went to his house the next day to get the life jackets. He had some of them laying on the driveway. I told him that was not all of the stuff. He said it was.

I said, "Bullshit."

I went into the garage to start looking for them. He pushed the button to close the garage door. Harmony ran over and stepped under the door and held it up. She yelled at him that he was not going to lock her mother in the garage. She yelled a whole bunch of stuff at him.

He called the police. I came out of the garage.

Harmony picked up Tiffany and said, "I'm taking Tiffany, and you will never see her again."

I had let Tiffany stay with him because he asked me if she could. I knew he loved her. He had been a lot nicer to her now that she was doing better at not pooping in the house.

As we got to the end of the driveway, Harmony grabbed his trash can and through it over. Trash went everywhere. I picked up the trash can and began to gather the trash. His brother Willey pulled up while I was doing it. I told him quickly what was happening. I then got in the car. Harmony was still out of control. He had a way of making her explode. She hated him.

I didn't give him any money. I was going to. It was in my pocket. I figured he got his money when he kept the jackets.

I decided then I was ready for the detective to submit my case to the DA. I called him early the next morning and told him to go forward. I was ready. I was tired of him doing my wrong.

WORLD'S BEST THERAPIST

I followed the Doctor's instructions. I went to the therapist appointment that they had set up for me. The lady seemed very nice. I saw her a couple of times. She had a very limited schedule. I couldn't work with it because I had missed way too much work. I asked if I could get a different therapist. I'm so glad that I did.

My new therapist Ellie is awesome. She is very kind, compassionate, and loving. She also speaks her mind. She doesn't go around anything. She tells you what it is and what it is not. I love that about her. She opened my eyes when they were closed.

At one point my insurance was not covering my therapy. She saw me anyways. She said I'm not going to just drop you. We will get things figured out. I have told her everything about what happened with Blane. I have talked at length about much of my life but still, have a lot more to tell her. She has been absolutely amazing giving me a lot of support on writing this book.

I told her the day I met her that I was going to write a book. I don't know if she believed me at the time that I would actually do it. She told me one day that she thought I would come for an appointment or two and that would be it.

I saw her for a little over six months before I started writing, but I kept saying I was going to.

She would say, "I know you are. You can do it."

She gave me her number in case I needed to call her due to what I was writing about. She is there for me no matter what.

When I got her as a therapist, I was blessed with a guardian angel.

FAMILY VACATION

I needed something to look forward to. I was beginning to get depressed when I got out of the hospital. I saw nothing in my future. I had no goals or desire to reach any if I had them. I would go to work come home and sleep. I did that day after day. I didn't want to be around anybody.

Sheryl would work with me and then on the weekend if she didn't hear from me she would show up at my door to see how I was doing. She was always texting and calling.

She said, "You're my best friend. I'm not going to let anything happen to you. So just get used to me popping in." I loved her so much.

I decided to plan a trip to California. I had never taken my granddaughters on a vacation. I began planning it. That helped with my mood. It also gave me something to get excited about.

I went to see Blane a few days before my trip. I asked him not to call me while I was gone. I told him that I needed time with my family without interruptions. I also told him I needed time to heal from everything that had been happening.

He said, "Okay I won't bother you."

I went into the kitchen. He followed me in there. He grabbed my hand and started to drag me to the bedroom.

I said, "No."

He continued to pull. I dropped to the floor and told him, "Stop. I don't want to do this."

He let go of my hand then walked to the family room. He was cold and distant. I just looked at him, and then I left.

I wanted to take Bennett, but he was in a treatment program, and they wouldn't let him go.

It was Harmony, Elizabeth, Anna, Kayden, and myself. I really didn't want Kayden to go, but Harmony really wanted her boyfriend to come. So, I let him come. We drove down in my minivan.

We had only been on the road for four hours when I picture popped up on my Facebook showing me a memory from 2013. It was a picture of Dave and me on the boat holding up a fish. We were driving past the exit for that lake just as it came through. I thought how strange is that. In the same place, just a couple of years later and it was not planned.

Blane and I had talked about that picture not to long before that because we couldn't find it. I battled with myself. I wanted to send it to him only because I know how important his Dad was to him. I didn't want to send it because I didn't want to have contact. I ended up sending it to him. He didn't respond. Which I kind of expected after our last encounter.

The next day he sent me a friend request on Facebook. Once again, another battle with myself. I did except against my better judgment.

Elizabeth, my oldest granddaughter, slept most the time we were driving. We would tease her that she slept most of the trip away. She was the lucky one. She would wake up, and we would be there.

Anna got bored during the driving times. Always asking the famous questions, "Are we there yet? How much longer?" We would try to distract her with games.

We all took turns with the radio. Everybody liked different stuff.

We stayed at my girlfriend Judy's house. It was a tight squeeze but we'll worth it. I always stay with her when I go to Vegas.

We walked the strip. I took lots of cool pictures of the kids. They were having a blast. I even stepped out of my comfort zone and danced with some street performer.

That night we were going to go to Freemont Street. Anna complained that she didn't feel good. She wanted to stay at the house. Harmony and Kayden volunteered to stay with her. She was faking. Not long after we left, she told Harmony she just didn't want to go. That really pissed Harmony off she had been looking forward to going.

Judy had some extra tickets for the water park. Judy, myself and my two granddaughters spent the day at the water park. I got adventurous and went on the water slides with my granddaughters. I wanted to show them a good time, so I got involved in the activities.

Judy had found a pair of sunglasses and gave them to Elizabeth. A Hispanic kid came up to her and said, "Those are mine." He was really rude.

Elizabeth said, "No there not."

Judy and I just stood there not knowing what to do.

Then the guy said, "There is a scratch on them that I made, I'll make a scene if you don't give them back to me."

Elizabeth said, "Whatever." Then she thrust them towards him. He took them and walked away. We all just started laughing. We started making jokes about it. I was finally starting to feel human again.

We left the next morning for California. I was low on funds from not working due to my mental breakdown. I asked my ex who lives in California if we could stay with him. He said that he would like that, but his house was not big enough for all of us. He took it upon himself to rent two hotel rooms for us.

We had some major problems in our relationship, but that had been 27 years ago. It seems like all my relationships have been full of turmoil and cheaters. He is my oldest son's father. He has grown into a wonderful man. He was very busy while we were there, so I only saw him the first night for a short time. I don't know if he knows how grateful I am that he was able to do that for us. I hope to someday pay him back tenfold.

The first day their we went to the beach. It was absolutely beautiful. The girls buried each other in the sand. I think that is what every child does when they go to the beach. They were playing so well together.

I sat there and watched them play. It was so peaceful. The seagulls flying overhead and the sound of the crashing waves. I could just sit there forever.

Then I got a text from Blane. He wanted to know what I had done with his battery charging machine that I had bought him for Christmas. I called him and told him I didn't touch it. I gave him some ideas where he could check for it.

A few hours later he texted me and apologized for accusing me of taking it. He had taken it to a job and left it in his brother Willy's truck. I think he was just looking for a reason to contact me.

I brushed it off. I wasn't going to let him ruin my trip. I was bound and determined to have a good time; to show my family a good time.

We went to universal studios. We managed to ride all the rides and see all the shows that we wanted to see. We had lunch at one of their snack shacks. They under cooked Kayden's hamburger. It made him sick. I was not about to pay that ridiculous price for a hamburger that was raw, so I went up to talk to the manager. He was very pleasant and refunded me for that burger. Unfortunately, that did not get rid of Kayden's tummy ache.

I took my kids to visit my family in Compton. They didn't believe me when I told them I had lived there.

We met up with Shelley at her beauty parlor then walked across the street to Mrs. Talker's apartment. We visited for quite a while. Shelley told them about the rapper's that used to live near the houses we grew up in. They were really intrigued.

She drove us by the rap star's, house who died of aids. She said his mama still lived there. I showed them my old house from my child hood and the school I went to. They didn't think that very interesting.

We dropped Kayden off at the airport. He had to go back to work. They wouldn't let him take the whole week off. It worked out good. I got to spend time with just my three girls.

My friend Denny lives in Simi Valley. We went up to stay with him for a couple of days. He had a beautiful room and had plenty of space for us to stay. We talked about Blane.

He said, "I didn't trust him from the minute I met him. Something just didn't feel right. Then when he hit on my friend it just confirmed my feelings. I'm glad you are moving on with your life you deserve so much better."

I said, "Your right I do."

We had planned ahead of time to go to Magic Mountain. It is an amusement park that is close to Denny's house. They are known for some of the best roller coasters. We were so excited about going. It ended up being one of the hottest days of our vacation.

We stood in a couple of lines for a long time. It was almost our turn on one of the roller coasters. We had been in line a long time. We were miserable. Sweat was rolling down our foreheads. Our mouths were dry and very thirsty. Then they closed the ride down. I was furious. We had been at the park for several hours and only been on one ride.

We talked amongst us and decided to leave and go to the beach. First, I wanted to let the management know that I had spent a large amount of money to come to their park. How disappointed I was with my visit. I told the gentleman behind the counter. I was nice about it even though I was very pissed off. He was very apologetic. He gave us several get in the front of the line vouchers. We decided to use them before we left.

We got Anna to go on one of the rides. She didn't have a chance to see what it was we just rushed her up to the front and put her on it. It was the largest one there. She would have never ridden it if she had known. I sat next to her. She was okay at first. Then she wasn't.

She started to cry when she saw how high up it was going. I told her it would be okay. She screamed as we went down. She got off and said that was fun. I asked you want to go on it again?

She said, "NO." real fast.

We went to get on another ride with our pass. It was temporarily closed. We gave the passes away. We left the park and went to the beach where we spent the rest of the day to early evening. That was much more enjoyable than Magic Mountain.

The last day and a half of our vacation were spent in Big Bear. We stayed with my niece and her kids. It was the first time all the cousins had met. My niece had a lot of animals, and both of my grandchildren loved petting and holding them. My two older brothers came over for a barbecue. It was a lot of fun.

The drive home was sad none of us wanted the trip to end. We had such a great time. No fights. Well, Harmony and Kayden had a few but not the girls. I'm looking forward to the day when I can go on another vacation with all of my family. I think that would be so much fun. I'm going to make that one of my dreams. I believe dreams come true. So now I just need to make it happen. Nothing happens in our lives unless we reach for it and believe. So I am reaching.

I went to see Bennett the weekend after we got back. He hated his new program. I thought the place he was staying in was disgusting. It was filthy. The staff didn't even introduce themselves to me. I didn't tell Bennett my opinion of the place. He had earned a pass, so we drove to Provo to go to the mall. The place he was staying was located in a small town, and everything was closed due to the fact it was Sunday.

He earned a twenty-four-hour pass to come home the following weekend. They drove him down here along with several other clients. We met at Ream's on state street. I signed his paperwork and had to ask the staff about his meds.

Once we were at the house, he asked if he could go see his friends. I told him no. We argued about it. I had to go to work for a couple of hours. I told Bennett not to leave while I was gone. He didn't answer me. I left and went to work. I was shocked when I got home. I thought for sure he would be gone, but he wasn't.

Later that evening I went to his room and told him I was going to bed. I gave him a hug and went out to my room. I felt lips on my forehead. I screamed as I was sitting up. "Get away from me."

Standing there in front of me was Bennett. He looked crushed. He had tears welling up in his eyes. He said, "I love you, mom. I just wanted to come tell you that, but you were asleep."

I said, "Come here." He sat next to me. I hugged him and explained to him that I didn't know that it was him. I said, "I love you and would not have have told you to get away from me."

We hugged each other tightly. I didn't know, but that would be the last time I would see him for quite a while. I went into his room the next morning. He left me a note telling me how sorry he was. He just couldn't go back there. He would take care of himself and would contact me later. He told me he loved me and I shouldn't blame myself.

I sat on the bed and cried. Not again. I worry nonstop when he is on the streets. Every time my phone rings I fear that it is a call giving me bad news or when a cop car drive past my house and slows down. I'm afraid they are going to come to my house with the news that every parent dreads.

I decided then that if he contacted me, I would help him. I would not turn him in as long as I knew he wasn't using hard drugs. He did finally contact me. I saw him frequently and tried to convince him to turn himself in. I'm his mother, and I broke the law, but I had to. I needed to be sure that he was eating and had what he needed. I knew that where he was staying was safe. Once I had gained his trust, he showed me.

A few months later he got picked up. His friend's Dad called and reported him. We started all over again with another program.

ENGLAND

When we got back, I went back to doing the same thing; hiding in my room. Work was about the only thing I did. I got a friend request on Facebook, I accepted. I talked to this guy for a while. He said he lived in England. He was an interior decorator. He sent me pictures of his work, showing me what he was working on, etc.

I finally asked him if we could talk on the phone. He told me he hated the way his voice sounded. I told him I didn't care. We talked on the phone. His voice was a little different but nothing to be ashamed of. He told me he wanted me to come to England he really wanted to meet me. We talked about me coming in September.

I kept waiting for him to ask me for money. I knew he was playing me, but I was lonely and having fun with it. He couldn't hurt me. He was just words on a screen and a voice on the phone. So, I played the game. He would tell me he wanted to spend his life with me. I would be thinking to myself. What bullshit. You don't even know me. I would laugh after our conversations; I was amused.

I hadn't talked to our seen Blane in several weeks. He called and asked how I was doing. I told him great, even though I had been isolating and feeling alone. I didn't want him to know that.

He asked if I wanted to come over for dinner. I knew better, but I went anyway. I'm a glutton for punishment. I got there and he was watching TV. I sat on the couch. He came over and sat by me. He leaned in to kiss me, and I stopped him. I said I can't.

He said, "You're seeing someone."

I said, "Yes, sort of."

I began to tell him about the guy I had been texting and talking to. He got a really sad look on his face. Which really threw me off because I really didn't think he cared. But it looked like maybe he did. He then began to tell me the guy was just a scammer. I already knew that but didn't want him to know that. He began to try and research him on the computer so that he could prove that he was just what he said he was. I went along with it.

After he was done, he started moving in on me again. I pushed him back. I told him, "I don't want to just stop." He did. For a while anyways.

After dinner, he started in again. Kissing me and hugging me I gave in. I'm human I just wanted to feel wanted and loved even though I knew he didn't love me.

The day final came. The guy in England told me he had just gotten a big contract in Asia. It was going to pay a lot of money. He was so excited. He told me he wanted to send copies of the contract to my email for safe keeping. Along with some other stuff.

I said that was fine. He said he wouldn't be talking to me for a few days because he would be traveling to that country. He would need time to get stuff in order once he was there.

He called me a couple of days later. He said he got there safely. Two days later he called me very upset. He said that Customs was holding his equipment because he didn't have enough to pay to get it through.

I said, "Oh really that sucks."

He said, "I can't start working until I have that stuff. I didn't realize that it would cost so much money to get set up. I ran out of all the money I brought. I can't access my accounts in England. Can you help me."

I said, "Yes I can. I can't do anything right this minute. I will go to the bank tomorrow."

He said, "Thank you, honey. I love you. I knew I could count on you."

I said, "You can always count on me."

I hung up the phone. I laid back on my bed. I started laughing. I said out loud, "What a dumb ass. You can count on me. For nothing. I'm not stupid."

He called me the next day. I asked him to give me the phone number for Customs that I would call them and pay them directly. I already knew it was a farce just wanted to hear him come up with more lies.

He told me he would call me back with the information. When he called back, he told me that they said they would only deal with him. I told him that is a government entity they wouldn't do that. He said well that is what they told me.

I told him I had talked to some people and they told me not to give you anything. I lied nobody told me that. I just knew better on my own. He got upset. He told me I shouldn't listen to other people. They don't care about you the way I do.

I thought to myself, "Really. You don't even know me. You're just a scammer looking to take advantage of someone who you think is vulnerable. What a loser." He hung on me.

A few minutes later he texted me telling me I got everything I deserved. I had confided in him about Blane. I told him the things that had happened. I felt safe because he couldn't use it against me and even if he told someone about it would not affect me.

He called me later and said he was sorry. He was just hurt because he was in love with me and thought I felt the same way. Then in his next breath, he asked me if he could ask me something. He asked me to promise to not tell my friends.

I said, "What is it you want to ask me."

He said, "I understand how you feel about sending the money. I have no way of accessing my accounts. Can you send me your information so I can open an account here in your name?"

I said, "No."

He said, "You're a piece of shit."

I hung up. Later that day I sent him a text telling him how pathetic he was. I told him that I hoped that someday he would meet some of the people he had ambushed and taken to the cleaners. I also told him that I hope that God would step into his life and let him see and feel some of the devastation that he has caused. I told him that I would be praying for him.

He sent back a snide remark. I just laughed. That was the end of him.

THE GIRL

Summer was just flying by. I slept through a lot of it. I never called Blane. He was the one who always made contact. I didn't want him to be able to say in court that I was chasing him. I was doing my best to move on with my life. I would tell my therapist about the times I did see him because I needed her to know everything. I wanted to get healthy again; to move forward with my life.

I hadn't heard anything from the detective or the DA. I began calling the detective. I called him constantly. He didn't answer, and he didn't return my calls. I wanted to know what was going on with my case. He finally called me back and told me the DA declined the charges.

He said, "Haven't they contacted you."

I said, "No I haven't heard anything. No letter or phone call."

I don't remember anything else from the conversation because I was pissed. Once again, the system has done me wrong.

It was in August when he called and asked me if I would like to go to dinner and a movie at Brewvies. I agreed to go. He picked me up at my house.

We ordered some food at Brewvies. I also ordered a Long Beach which is the same as a long island ice tea except that it is made with cranberry juice.

Brewvies is a movie theater that only allows people twenty-one or older to come in because they serve alcohol.

As I walked into the theater, my purse accidental ran across the shelf they had in front of the seats to hold drinks. I knocked over several drinks. Oops. I had to hold my laugh inside. I apologized to the people.

Blane asked them what they were drinking and then went and got them new drinks. I didn't ask him what they cost, and I didn't offer to pay for them either. I figured he could take care of it. It's the least he could do for all the hell he had put me through.

I drank my drink in record time. I just felt like I wanted to escape. He bought me another one. By the time we left, I was pretty buzzed. I closed my eyes as we were driving. I had assumed he was just going to take me home because we were so close to my house.

When he turned the car off, I opened my eyes. We were in his driveway. Before we opened up the car doors, a young girl appeared. She came up to his window. She was so excited to see him. When she saw me, she seemed very hurt.

We got out of the car. She followed us into the house. Blane introduced us. She asked him for a cigarette. He gave her a few of them. He told her that she needed to go home, that he was going to be spending some time with me. She looked so sad and hurt. I tried to judge her age. I wasn't sure how old she was. I thought that she might be about sixteen. After she had left I asked Blane how old she was.

He said, "She is eighteen. I would not talk to her otherwise. I'm not willing to go back to prison for anybody. I hired her to water the grass for me. Her family bought Dad's rental house down the street."

I said, "Okay."

We sat on the couch for a bit. I started to doze off. He grabbed me by the arm and lifted me up off the couch. I didn't say anything. He led me to his room by the arm.

Once we were in there, he picked me up and placed me on the bed. I was really buzzed. My head started spinning. I felt like I was going to be sick. I said I need to go to the bathroom. I went in there and sat on the toilet facing the sink. If I was going to throw up it was going to be in the sink I was not putting my head in the toilet. I sat there for several minutes.

He came into the bathroom to see if I was okay. He led me back to the room. He started to undress me while I was standing up. Then everything went black. I must have passed out. Sometime later he was nudging me telling me I needed to get dressed. I got dressed still feeling intoxicated.

After I was done getting dressed he took me home. I felt horrible the next day. I hadn't got that drunk in a long time. I know we had sex because I was sore and well I know his scent. How can someone have sex with a person that is not really there? I wonder if he enjoyed it because I sure don't remember it.

A SKANK

I had a job that needed some special cleaners that I had left on the shelf next to Blane's garage. I decided to stop by and get it without calling him. I grabbed the stuff off the shelf. Then I decided to see if the door to the house was unlocked. I turned the knob and opened the door. I stepped inside. A woman dressed in pajamas came walking out of the kitchen.

She was about five feet six. She was extremely skinny with long stringy blondish brown hair. She had several missing teeth; she was very wrinkly. She looked like she had been through the ringer. My first impression of her is that she was a tweaker. My first impression was correct. She introduced herself. She said she was an old friend of Blane's. That he was just helping her out with a place to stay.

I told her I didn't care. That I was not with Blane and what he did had nothing to do with me.

I texted Blane after I left. I told him I had met his skank. I texted him that she looked disgusting, that he had stooped pretty low. He texted back with his famous word. Whatever. She is just a friend.

didn't talk to him for several weeks after that. I really didn't talk to him very often anyways, so it really wasn't a big deal.

MY BIRTHDAY AGAIN

September is back again. It seems like the year has just flown by.

I hadn't talked to Blane for a few weeks. I have a job that I do on call for a bed and breakfast. I had gotten Blane hired on to do his repairs on the house. My employer didn't want him going in on his own, so he had me meet him there to let him in to do work. I had some deep cleaning that I needed to do so when he called and asked me to let Blane in I did.

Blane was working on a door jam downstairs. I went up to the top floor and began washing the blinds. Suddenly Blane was behind me. He grabbed me off the ladder and laid me on the bed. I froze. I didn't say anything. He laid on top of me and began kissing me hard. He then stood up and took off his pants. Then he grabbed my pants and pulled them off. I wanted to scream stop. I wanted to get up and run. I counted the stripes on the comforter. It was quick thank God. I don't know what was wrong with me. I just froze.

When he was done, he went back downstairs and finished his project. I hated myself for not standing up to him. I didn't say stop. I didn't say no. I sat there and cried because I hated myself for letting it happen. When am I going to get a backbone? When will I be able to not answer my phone when he calls. I hate myself for being so weak. I am stronger than I was before but not strong enough.

He finally got his job done. He came to tell me he was done and leaving. I didn't look at him. I didn't want him to see that my eyes were red and swollen from crying. He is so insensitive that I didn't want to hear him say those words again. "What are you boobing about?" He had said that to me so many times I just didn't need to hear it again.

I went to Sheryl's house after he left. She only lived a block from where this house is. She could tell that I was upset. I didn't want to tell her what happened because she would become very upset. She did mention that she saw that Blane was at the house. I told her he had to do a job for the owner. She just looked at me with love and concern in her eyes. She wasn't stupid she knew something had happened while I was there with him.

Three days later it was my birthday. I took myself out to eat. I waited to see if he was going to call or text me Happy Birthday. He never did. I was angry. Actually, I was hurt. I don't even know why I should I let it bother me.

The next day he came to my house to pick up some money from my roommate. He had been doing some work on the house she was going to be moving into. I told her he didn't call me. I was going to stay in my room when he came because I didn't want to see him. She told me I should be in the house when he came. I was sitting at the kitchen table when she let him in the front door.

He said, "How was your Birthday"?

I said, "Fuck you. Like you even give a shit."

He said, "Wow. What's wrong with you?"

I said, "You couldn't even call me or text me Happy Birthday?"

He said, "I did."

He came over to me and opened his phone and said, "See here it is." As he showed it to me, he realized he sent it to the wrong Julee.

He said, "Sorry I sent it to the wrong person."

Then he walked out and got in the truck with his brother Willey. I went out to the truck. I went to his window, and I told him he needed just to leave me alone. You are obviously seeing someone. I told him my roommates would be out by the end of the month and I would contact him about getting my furniture that was still in the house. I didn't have room for it, so I had left it there.

My roommate told me he had been seeing some girl. She called him all the time when he was at her house working. She thought that I knew, but obviously, I didn't.

The funny thing about this girl, is that it was someone he had been with years before. He introduced her to me while we were still living together in our house. She works at the local grocery store. I had commented to him that I thought something was going on. He told me he would never go out with her again. She was a nasty piece of work. She slept with anybody that would get her high. She lied to me all the time, and she cheated on me. He was just being her friend because she was going through a hard time. The guy she was with, was doing her dirty. He just wanted to give her moral support.

I thought to myself yeah right Blane. I don't believe you. It is really funny how he ended up with her. Poor girl doesn't know what kind of man she's got. She will though; once she reads this book.

STD

It was about a week after my Birthday when Blane called me. He began to ask me questions about the time I had gone to the gynecologist. I told him it was because of my bladder. I asked him why he wanted to know. He told me that I had given him an STD.

I went off. I told him I hadn't been with anyone but him. If he had one, he contracted it somewhere else. I asked him if I needed to go to the doctor.

He said, "Yes you should."

I told him that he was a piece of shit for trying to blame me for something like that. I hung up the phone. I was furious. I immediately called my doctor and set up an appointment.

I went to my appointment. The doctor said we should check for everything. I peed in a cup and gave blood. She told me she would call me with the results and if need be, she would have a prescription sent to my pharmacy.

She called me a couple of days later. He had given me an STD. I was boiling. I cried. I decided that I needed to let his girlfriend know what he had given me. He told me one thing, but there were two.

I messaged her on Facebook. I told her what he gave me. She didn't believe me. She thought I had been the one to give it to him. She treated me like I was dirty. That really made me angry. She finally sent me a message saying that I need to leave them alone. They are happy together and that I needed to get on with my life. If she only knew that he was always the one to make contact. I told her fine and didn't bother her again. He obviously hadn't started doing to her what he had done to me. Unless she too is living in denial of what he is doing to her.

I became very bitter. I couldn't stop thinking about ways to get even with him. I had all kinds of scenarios playing out in my head. I wanted to hurt him just like he had hurt me. I wanted him to suffer a slow painful death. I would get so angry at times I would just cry.

I felt like it was not fair. How could he move on so easily? I don't think that I will ever be able to have another relationship and that made me very angry. I'm destined to be alone for the rest of my life because of the things he did to me. Yet here he is in a relationship. I felt like life just wasn't fair. I had to do several sessions with my therapist to try to deal with the anger. I was so angry that I even talked to someone about hurting him. I just wanted him to feel that feeling of helplessness and be unable to stop that object from penetrating.

After I had talked to that person, I decided I needed to start praying again. I knew it wasn't the right thing to do, but the need for revenge was so great. I opened up my Bible to read some scriptures. God put the right scripture in front of my face. I knew I had to call that person and cancel what I had planned.

I began to pray constantly. I prayed that he would find true happiness. That all of his dreams would come true.

I asked God to give me a forgiving heart. I had learned a long time ago in a twelve-step program that in order to forgive someone who has harmed you and that you are holding a resentment against you need to pray for them to have a better life. So, that is what I was doing. I didn't want to continue feeling the rage and hate that I was harboring towards him.

FIRST ATTEMPT AT DATING

I was messaged on Facebook by a guy I didn't know. He asked to be friends. I looked at his profile. Some of the friends on his friend's list were also my friends from church. I decided to friend him.

We talked a few times. He invited me to his house for dinner. He told me he hadn't been working very much and couldn't afford to go out. I understood how that could be so; I said that would be fine. I got to his house. He hadn't even started to prepare dinner. He was like I don't know how to cook. I jumped in and found stuff to make spaghetti.

After dinner, we watched a movie. He was a gentleman the whole time.

He invited me to see his son perform at a club in Ogden. He had two extra tickets, so I took Tera, the lady who had been staying at my house. It was not my type of music. It was rap. If I had known that I wouldn't have gone. His ex-wife was there. It was so funny. I knew her. She had come to mine and Blane's house when we were still together. She came with my good friend who was demonstrating some cookware that he was selling. We chatted for a few.

I left town the next week. He texted me a couple of times while I was gone.

ARIZONA

My son James, and his girlfriend Kennedy moved to Arizona at the beginning of the summer. I hadn't gone to see them yet. He invited me to come down. I really needed to get away. I thought a change of scenery would be good for me.

I had been feeling better due to the fact that I had been reading a very healthy book. "Finding your purpose." I had also been watching all of the Pastors videos online. But when I got that ugly news from Blane about what he gave me I became very angry and resentful and couldn't shake it.

I told James I could come for a couple of days. He asked if I could try to stay longer so I arraigned it so I could stay for several days. I'm really glad that I did. I didn't realize how much I had missed him until I saw him.

The day he told me that they were moving, I had to hold back my tears. It was Mother's Day. We went out to dinner. I was happy for them because Kennedy had just gotten a big promotion, but all I could think was I'm losing my boy. I sobbed when I got home I knew that I had lost him.

They had rented a beautiful house. In a very nice neighborhood. Kennedy had to work the whole time I was there. James had taken time off so we could spend a lot of time together.

James and I went to the river, where we floated down on a raft that he had purchased that summer. It was beautiful. We saw wild horses standing in the water, cranes were in the bushes, and some were in the water. The weather was perfect. It was amazing. We talked about all kinds of stuff. It made me feel so good when he confided somethings to me. It had been so long since we had spent such quality time together. I had a close relationship with him at one point in time but lost it over the last several years. I felt closer to him that day than I had in a long time.

That night we had decided to go to the casino and play bingo. The three of us went. Kennedy won. She had also won the last time they went. I played on my phone so much that it died. James had a few drinks while we were there when we got in the car to head back to their house he decided to lay down in the back seat.

As we were driving down the freeway, we saw a car that was swerving. We didn't get close to him because we were afraid he might hit us. We followed him for a bit.

I said, "We should call 911".

Kennedy said, "You don't want to be one of those kind of people, do you?"

I responded, "I guess not."

My phone was dead, so I couldn't have called from mine. James phone had died that evening as well. I don't know if Kennedy's had a charge; it probably didn't. She had been playing on her phone too.

We tried to figure out what kind of car he was driving but we were too afraid to get close enough to see. Then he was gone from our view. A white truck that was behind us hurried around us and took off in a quickness. We assumed that he was either following this car or that maybe they were together.

We got off the freeway and turned onto a street that had two lanes going in our direction; then there was a big dirt medium in the middle with two lanes going the other direction on the other side. We drove for several miles when we saw a woman standing very close to the lane we were driving in.

She was frantic. You could tell there had been an accident. I yelled at Kennedy to pull over. She did. James and I jumped out of the car and ran down to the accident. The young women came running towards us. She thrust a phone into my hand. I handed it to James. I would have been no help to the 911 operator because I didn't even know where we were.

The young woman was screaming. "I can't find my sister."

I already knew that his sister was dead. As we were hurrying down to the scene of the accident, I saw her sister's hand. Several feet away from where the hand was I saw her leg from the knee down. I placed my hands on her arms and looked her in the eye. I asked her if she was okay. Are you injured anywhere? She was covered in blood. It must have been her sisters.

She said, "No. I need to find my sister."

I hated what I had to do, but she needed to know so that she would quite searching. I told her. "Your sister didn't make it. You need to quite looking for her."

She began to sob. My heart was breaking for her. I hugged her and told her how sorry I was. She walked over to the side of the road. I then opened the door to the back seat. The front door of the car had been taken by the car that hit them. There was a woman with a baby sitting back there. She was sobbing because she already knew that her friend had been hit and dragged away by the other car. After I was done seeing if she was okay, I got out of the car.

They had a minor fender bender with another car. They were standing out there talking when this happened. I asked the lady to go turn on the hazard lights of her car. They hadn't turned them on. It was a very dark road. We almost didn't see them when we went by. She turned on her lights and then got into her car to wait for the emergency crew.

During this time, James had been on the phone with 911. I could hear sirens in the distance. Several trucks arrived on scene. Several police cars showed up as we'll. They blocked off both sides of the highway. I just stood there in the middle of the highway looking down at all the lights.

I was numbed. "This couldn't be real," I thought. There was a slight breeze; I suddenly had goosebumps all over my body.

Kennedy had stayed in the car. She came walking up after the first responders had arrived. We just stood there waiting to see if anyone wanted to talk to us. No one approached us, so we left. Kennedy said we shouldn't have stopped.

I just looked at her in disbelief of what she had just said. They were people in need of assistance. How can you just ignore that? I didn't say that to her, but I thought it.

As we had walked back to the car I was looking at the ground, there were pieces of flesh everywhere. The rest of the ride home nobody spoke. I think we were all in disbelief of what had just happened.

I laid in bed that night for hours. I couldn't sleep. I was replaying everything in my head. If I had called would it had made a difference? Every time I closed my eyes, I would see that young lady waving her arms in desperation. I would see all the gore on the road. It was awful.

I had quite taking my dream suppressant medication that they had put me on while I was in the hospital. I would wake up screaming. Terrified and shaking. I decided then that when I got back home, I needed to start taking it again. I quit taking it because I wanted to start dreaming again. If I had to deal with some nightmares so be it, I missed dreams. Until I could deal with this new nightmare, I would have to take them.

My flight left the next afternoon.

They took me to the airport early so that they could go to the fair. We stopped at the gas station near the highway where the accident was. The clerk said the highway had been closed all night and had just barely opened back up. I bought a newspaper to see if anything had been put in the early addition. There was nothing. Several days later Kennedy sent me an article that they had put in the local paper.

The trip home seemed like it was taking forever. I really didn't want to go home. I had people staying in my house. I had told them several weeks before this trip that they had to move while I was gone. My other roommate informed me that they were still there and showed no signs of leaving.

I was also worried about the upcoming weekend. I had made arraignments with Blane to get the rest of my stuff. I didn't have a good feeling about it. I had not spoken to him since he had accused me of giving him the STD. I knew I was still holding a lot of anger inside. My fear was that I would do something I would regret.

HOME SWEET HOME

When I got home I could tell that I was missed; my dogs went nuts. They loved on me nonstop. I went to Sheryl's to get Tiffany. I knew that she would be well taken care of over there. She bought Tiffany a new toy. It was a long yellow thing with arms and legs. It would make a squeaking sound when she bit it. Tiffany loves that toy.

I really needed to see my best friend after what I had endured on my trip. We talked for hours. She was always great at making me feel better. She looked at things so differently than other people. She was just amazing.

Tara, her boyfriend, her son and the dog were still in my house. I had asked for her to be gone when I returned. She asked me if I could give them a little more time. She had helped my son when he was on the streets. She was always helping runaways. She had a big heart. The family had lost their home because the owners wanted to remodel it so that they could rent them for more money.

They had nowhere to go. I told them they could come stay with me while they were looking for a place. I told her that she couldn't bring people to stay at my house, no drug use of any kind. I also told her that her boyfriend could not drink at my house. I also let her know that her son could not be bringing all his buddies over. She had told me he was going to be staying with friends until they found a place. She said that would not be a problem. She said she would follow the rules.

I told her that she needed to start looking for a place immediately, that this was only temporary. They had been staying at my house for about a month when her son was starting stay with us. He brought his friends over several times. I told her that this is not a flop house. I let you know ahead of time that this was unacceptable. One morning I went downstairs to do laundry. She had people sleeping all over my basement.

There was a man sleeping on my couch. I grabbed hold of his leg. I began to shake it.

I said, "Wake up you fuckin' nigger. What the hell are you doing sleeping on my couch?"

He opened his eyes and looked at me. Then he jumped to his feet. He took his arms and wrapped them around me so tightly I could barely breathe.

He said, "I missed you, mom."

I hugged him back just as tightly and kissed him on his cheek.

I said, "I missed you too, son."

He said, "You scared the shit out of me."

I said, "I know," and we both started laughing.

It was one of Bennett's friends. I had not seen him in months. We sat on the back porch while we smoked. He told me about all his adventures.

'm not a racist person. I believe that everyone is equal. God created us in his image. I knew that Bennett's friend would not be hurt by what I said. He knew that I loved him and was only playing. I would have never said something like that if it was going to hurt him.

She started to drag stuff in; every time I would come home there would be more. She started putting things in my closet and rearranging my stuff. I told her several times to get all the stuff out. She just ignored me. I began getting very angry. This went on for several months.

It was now October. They had been at my house for three months. Their huge dog ruined my carpet. He bit my roommate twice. He bit me once. I was trying to tough it out so they could get on their feet. It got to the point that I just couldn't do it anymore. My son was supposed to come home around the first of December. I needed them out.

Tara and her boyfriend fought constantly. I would have to ask them to be quiet. I would tell them that not everybody wants to hear their drama. One day she came running to me. She was crying.

She said, "You need to stop Mich. He is throwing my stuff away."

I went to him and told him he could not throw her things away.

He said, "Do you want to see what I'm throwing away?"

I said, "Yes."

He walked over to their car. He pulled out a purse. He opened it in front of me.

He said, "This is what I'm throwing away."

It had several meth pipes in it along with some other paraphernalia. I was pissed. I went straight to her. I started screaming at her. I told her she was a piece of shit. That she was totally disrespectful. How could she use in my house? I'm sure I said a lot more than that.

She started saying, "Mich, was doing it too."

I was livid. I had to go to my room to calm down. If I didn't walk away, I might have really done them some harm.

She came to my room later that evening. She apologized and told me she hadn't used in the last week. That is why they were constantly fighting.

She told me they were really trying to find a place. She begged me to let her stay a little longer. I gave her a date to be out.

I said, "You have to leave on that date."

SECOND DATE

Al called and asked me out again. He wanted to know if I would like to come watch a movie. He had recently moved in with his son. He now lived in Magna. I didn't have anything planned, so I decided to go.

We were sitting on the couch watching the movie when he put his hand on top of mine. I immediately began panicking on the inside. I started sweating. My stomach felt like it was in knots. I wanted him to take his hand off of mine. It made me so uncomfortable. I said I needed to go to the restroom. When I came back, he was lying on the other couch with a blanket. He asked if I would like to lay down and get comfortable.

I said, "NO." Really fast.

He left the idea alone. I sat back down on the couch. As soon as the movie was over, I told him I had to go. He wanted me to spend the night. I told him that I was not that kind of girl. I gave him a quick hug.

I was a nervous wreck all the way home. I knew then that it would be a long time before I would feel comfortable with a man. I was destined to stay single. Just having him touch my hand sent me into a panic.

He was supposed to help me get my stuff from Blane's house on Sunday. I talked to him that morning. He told me he would call me back shortly to let me know where to pick him up. He never called me back that day.

I'm glad that he didn't help it would have made things more difficult.

A few days later a good friend of mine from church called me. He had heard that I was talking to this guy. He told me he was bad news. I had been warned like that once before and didn't listen. We'll I would like to say that this time I listened. I haven't spoken to Al, and I don't plan on ever speaking to him again.

SHE SNAPPED

The day had finally come. It was time for me to get my furniture out of the house we purchased together. I hadn't seen or talked to him since our last conversation when he blamed me for giving him that STD. I was still seething with anger. I just wanted to kick him right where it hurts. I knew that I couldn't do it because I didn't want to go to jail. I know he would just love to see me get arrested. I wasn't going to give him that.

I had reserved a moving truck. I told them what I had, and they said the truck they were giving me would have more than enough room. They were wrong. I was pissed and believe me when I returned the truck I let them know.

I went to pick up the truck with my roommate. He was supposed to drive over to his friend's house and then come right over. I waited for an hour and a half for them to arrive.

When they finally got there, I started yelling at him. "What took you so long? You knew that this was not going to be an easy thing to do."

He apologized and said his friend wasn't ready when he got there.

When I got to Blane's house, nobody was there. I had brought his ladder that I had at my house. I took down all the camera's that I had put up when I had my protective order against him. He arrived just a few minutes after I had finished. The first thing that came out of his mouth was "You're not taking the camera's."

I said, "I already took them down."

He said, "That's it, we're not doing this."

His sister said, "Yes we are. We need to get this done and over with."

He said, "Whatever."

His sister was the one who told me to buy those security cameras. When I had the protective order, she told me he was dangerous, and I needed to have those to make sure he didn't come into the house while I was there alone. There was a gate in the backyard that he could enter through without anyone knowing. She told me a lot of things during that time. She had me scared to death. She even talked to the Jordan police department and told them I wasn't safe. That he needed to be removed from the house, he was staying in that was only two doors down.

I tried explaining to her, what he had given me. She said that didn't matter. We needed to just get my stuff out. She was being a real bitch.

said, "Your brother is a piece of shit."

She said, "He is my brother. I love him. I'm here to help him. So, let's get this done."

Now, I'm really pissed. Of course, she supports him. She just wants to get Dad's estate settled so she can get her money. She is a two-faced liar. She is just looking out for herself. None of her siblings can stand her.

Then he walked in the back door. I followed behind him. His sister was right on our heels. She had her nose in every conversation. If we said anything to each other, she would butt right in. She would tell us to quit talking to each other. She actually made the whole situation a lot more stressful. She brought her fifteen-year-old son.

When Blane and I would start saying mean things to each other, she would say my son doesn't need to hear this. I thought to myself then why did you bring him. You knew this was not going to be an easy deal.

I told Blane that I wanted my two end tables that I had purchased from our neighbor when she was having a yard sale. They matched the coffee table that was given to us when we bought the house.

He said, "You're not taking anything out of the living room." The way he said it gave me chills. It sounded so evil.

I said, "You will eventually pay for everything you've done to me."

He yelled out to his sister that was in the living room. She just threatened me.

I said, "Whatever Blane. You're a liar."

A short time later we were in the living room. His sister had stepped outside.

Blane said, "You better watch your back." He waited until we were alone to threaten me. That's just the kind of person he is.

I said, "I'm not afraid of you."

He said, "You should be."

I went outside. I felt sick to my stomach. I have heard about some of the ways he has gotten even with people. I knew that he might make good on his threats.

Tara got there shortly after Blane and his sister. He wouldn't let her come into the house to help. I said, "I brought her to help so we could get this done quickly."

He said, "I don't care. I don't want her in here."

I just shook my head. I went outside and told her he was being his normal douche bag self.

She said, "That's okay. I will just hang out and help load the truck when it arrives.

I was glad she was there because things were getting heated.

We put a bunch of my stuff out on the front lawn while we waited for the truck to arrive. It finally got there. Blane's sister went up to my friends and started yelling at them that there better not be any problems.

My roommate said, "We don't want any. We are just here to get Julee's stuff". She calmed right down. We started loading the truck.

They loaded the truck, but there was not enough room for everything. They had to go drop it off and come back.

While they were gone, I sat in my van on the street. I was facing the girl's house. I thought to myself. I wonder did he give her the STD. I decided that I was going to take a little walk down there to find out. I knocked on the door.

A middle-aged woman answered. I told her that I was Blane's ex-girlfriend. I asked if her daughter was home. She told me she wasn't. She said that she was actually her foster child. That she was only seventeen and that she suffered some mild retardation which made her slower than other's her age.

I was stunned. I then began to explain to this woman that he was registered sex offender. He had her working for him which put her at risk. I told her about the night she showed up at his house. She was stunned. She said she didn't let her go out that late. She must have snuck out. I wondered to myself, how many other times has she snuck out and gone to his house. I let her know that she needed to report this to his parole officer. I told her she needed to take her to the doctor to be checked.

I thought to myself after I left, "I got you now, you stupid son-of-a-bitch. They have to do something about this." He put that girl in a position that gave him power and control. He was her employer which is kind of like the situation of him being the step-father of his other victims.

I waited for the truck to return. It seemed like they were taking forever. While I was waiting for them Blane's girlfriend showed up. She is short, dark hair with a funky mullet hair style, dark skin.

Once they got back, we began to load the rest of the stuff. I asked Blane where the handles were to my refrigerator. His sister butted right in. I told her to shut the fuck up. I had enough of her. Blane slammed the door.

He said, "You have all you're going to get."

I still had stuff in there. I got pissed. I started yelling loudly so that the neighbors could hear. I yelled that he was a child rapist, he likes to rape women. I yelled that he was just like his father. Having kids all over the place. The apple doesn't fall too far from the tree.

His sister came flying out the door. She got right in my face. Telling me, she was going to Fuck me up. I just looked at her. I was as cool as a cucumber.

I said, "Go ahead hit me."

She then chest bumped me. I laughed. She was getting angrier. I was in control. She had totally lost it. Blane and his nephew came running out. They grabbed her and dragged her back into the house. They told her to calm down we don't need the cops out here.

I stood on the lawn in front of the big window. I looked in the window. They were all standing there watching me. I looked right at his girlfriend. She looked at me like she was something special. Like she had won the prize. If she only knew what she had. I felt sorry for her. She didn't know what she was getting herself into.

On my way home, I realized I didn't get my coffee table that Joe had given me. It was in the living room that he would not let me enter. I was pissed. That table has so many memories. I was going to get it back one way, or the other.

The next day I called his parole officer. He had gotten a new one. Larry gave me his number. I called several times. He didn't return my call. I decided a few days later that I was going to have to go down there. I went down to adult probation and parole. His Parole Officer was not in. They had me meet with another parole officer.

I began telling him about the young girl. I told him how his last Parole officer had put a no contact order in his parole stipulations and how he had violated it several times by seeing me. It seemed like he didn't care. I was more concerned about telling them about the girl that I had forgotten to mention my stuff. I don't think they ever investigated what I had told them about the girl. It's like they just don't care. They don't want to do any more work than they have too. I also think because I'm the ex-girlfriend they blew it off. They probably figured I was just trying to be vindictive.

I called his parole officer the next day to tell him about the stuff Blane still had that belonged to me. He told me to text him a list of the things. I did. I waited several days to hear back from him.

I finally called him back to see what and if he was going to do to help me get my stuff. He didn't answer. I called multiple times and sent him texts. He never responded. I just gave up. I decided they weren't going to help me. It would probably be too much work for them. He couldn't even be human enough to call and tell me that. Just ignored the situation. Just like all the other stuff they ignore.

It makes no sense to me. They group all these guys together in half-way houses. The convicts become friends. They share who their Parole officers are. The Parole Department believes that these guys just stop being friends. They keep in contact, and if they have the same parole officer, they let their buddy know if he has come to their house so that they can be prepared if they stop by theirs or they make sure to be gone before they come to their house.

The thing is, the people that these monsters have relationships with end up knowing things that are important. They hold onto them but eventually have to let them out. They should learn to listen to us. These predators turn us into their victims by the things they do to us. But eventually, we get to the point where enough is enough. I was at that point.

The sad thing about that young girl is that she may be walking around with a disease in her body. I don't think her foster mother took me seriously. She was probably afraid to say anything because she is afraid to lose her meal ticket. The money was probably more important than the welfare of that child. I have wanted to go over to her house to find out but feel it's best not to.

I did what I thought was the right thing. I hope that they did too.

GOING TO GREAT LENGTHS

The date was approaching. I started reminding Tara that she and her family had to be out of my house. I felt that I had to keep saying something because they had not left the last few times they were supposed to go. I told her a couple of days before the day she was to go and she screamed at me. "I KNOW."

I yelled back at her and said, "Don't yell at me. I have helped you out long enough."

The morning came for them to move. I hadn't seen any movement, so I went downstairs. It was ten a.m. I knocked on their door.

I said, "You guys need to get up. I need you to start getting your stuff out."

She yelled at me, "I know what time it is."

I went upstairs. I was standing in the driveway when she came out with Oscar. I told her they need to start getting their things together. She looked at me and said, "We're not leaving."

I said, "Yes you are. You are getting out of my house today."

She said, "No were not. There is nothing you can do about it."

I thought to myself. Really. I already had a feeling that she was going to pull this. So, I did my research. I was going to have to put my plan into action.

She headed across the street with Oscar so that he could use the restroom. I went into my room and put on my thick winter jacket. I needed to make sure that my arms were protected. I was a little worried about my face, but at the same time, I didn't care. I just needed these people out. They were making my life a living hell. I also had my boy coming home in December, and I didn't want them there.

She was heading back towards the house. I went out of the yard into the middle of the street. I got in her face and began yelling at her. I was moving my arms around. Oscar did exactly what I thought he would do. He started growling and then latched on to my arm. I started yelling. "Your dog is attacking me." I got him to let go. I told her not to take him back into my yard. I was calling animal control.

My neighbor was sitting in his car. I walked up and asked him if he saw the dog attack me.

He said, "Yes."

I waited for the animal control. She had put Oscar in her car. I went into the house. She began screaming at me; making all kinds of threats. I remained calm because I knew that they had no choice but to leave.

I knew that I had a right not to have that dog on my property. I also knew that he would not be in trouble. I made sure he would not be punished for his actions. He was on a leash, and I was in his personal space. I would never put the dog at risk because I love dogs. Also, it wasn't his fault; his owner's put him in the living situation he was in.

The animal control showed up. She told me that Tara had licensed her dog to my address a couple months earlier. I was shocked. It didn't matter though. She still told Tara that she could not take him onto my property.

I ended up having to pay, to have my dog's licenses renewed but it was well worth the fifty dollars to get them out.

They started putting stuff in their car. I just stood there and smiled. I make things happen. It's something you have to learn when you have been taken advantage of. I have learned over the years that sometimes you have to go to great lengths to make things happen. You can't just sit and wait you have to go after whatever it is you want.

I canceled work that day. I wanted to be there when they were getting their stuff out. They left and didn't come back all day. I was furious. I had missed a whole day of work.

Her boyfriend and her son came back the next day. They put all of their stuff on the driveway. They packed as much as they could in the car. She had been arrested for an old DUI warrant. I thought that was kind of funny. That's what she gets for treating me like shit. I guess Karma has a way of coming back to bite you.

They never came back for the rest of the stuff. I called them multiple times to come get it out of my driveway. They didn't respond. After a couple of weeks, I threw it away. It was mostly just junk she had drug in. None of it was worth anything.

I called Sheryl and told her what I had done. She was so happy that I had gotten them. She knew how miserable they had made me. We brainstormed several other scenarios on how to get them out.

I'm just glad that I was finally able to cleanse myself of them. They were toxic.

SCHOOL BEGINS

I started school on November 1, 2016. My daughter thought it would be good for me to go back to school. I totally agree with her. I'm going to school to be a master esthetician. I am getting too old to clean houses for a living. My body is constantly in pain. Somedays I don't feel like I'm going to be able to finish. It's just starting to be too much for me to handle. I'm going to have to stick it out for a while, but I'm looking forward to the day that I don't have to do it. I do have a few clients that I will continue to work for only because I have grown to love them and consider them more than just a client.

I was really afraid of starting school. I am socially awkward. I don't make friends very easily. I tend to push people away. I don't even realize that I'm doing it. I was very uncomfortable the first couple of months. I had no confidence in myself. I didn't feel like I was capable of doing the things they were teaching.

One Saturday afternoon I got booked for a manicure. I was exhausted. I had already done several facials. The lady sat down. She was already in a bad mood. She was a last-minute booking, so it took me a few minutes to get set up. I tried to ignore her bad attitude. Some of the other girls saw how rude she was to me. They notified the instructor. She came over to see what was going on. The lady started saying very mean things to me. I told her I had done more pedicures than manicures.

She said, "I wouldn't let you near my feet. This obviously isn't your calling."

I thought to myself. Your right lady it's not. I'm not here to learn nails. That's not what I came here for. My instructor told her that she couldn't talk to her students that way. The lady got even more irate. She stormed out of the building without even paying.

I felt bad for half a second. I then went about my business. I went downstairs to do my cleaning. One of the owners of the school started looking for me. She wanted to make sure I was okay after the way the client treated me. I told her I was fine.

I'm glad to say that has changed. I now know that I can do whatever they put in front of me. I have to practice some of the things so I can gain speed.

I enjoy doing the European facials. I take advantage of it. I pray before I go in to work on the client and while I am giving them their treatment I pray for them. I hope that when I'm giving them this service, they are feeling relaxed and enjoying it and that it helps them in their spiritual walk.

WHY HER GOD?

I needed to practice painting nails. I asked Sheryl if I could give her and her daughter manicures. She said that would be awesome. She was so excited about having me do it. She rarely got her nails done so she said this would be a treat. I did a pretty good job but still wasn't happy with the way they turned out. She said they looked great. Sheryl wouldn't have said they looked like crap even if they did. I told her that I would do it again in a few weeks after I had time to practice. I never got the chance.

Sheryl had neck surgery. She introduced me to a friend of her's that she had met at church. She wanted to make sure I had someone to help me work while she was recovering.

Stacy turned out to be a very nice lady. She helped me when I needed her. She and Sheryl had gotten close in the few months that they knew each other.

In mid-November, Sheryl called me and asked for a ride to go cash a check.

She had crashed her car the previous weekend and now had no transportation. I was used to taking Sheryl to her appointments, shopping and wherever else she needed to go. For years, she didn't have a car. I liked to take her to do her errands it gave us time to spend together other than the times we worked.

That day I went over she looked like she had been crying. She was upset. She told me that her husband had been cheating on her. She told me he got a text from some other woman. I looked at his phone. It was a message that had been texted to him about having a good time this weekend. I called the number. It was a promo thing from a casino.

He had been driving a truck but was now in the hospital. He had been diagnosed with stage three cancer. I assured her that it was not another woman. It was just an advertisement. She had been so upset. Lately, she told me she didn't know what she was going to do if he died. She was scared.

I took her to cash a check. Then we went to my house. I had cleaned out my food pantry and had a lot of can food that I would not be using. I gave it to her. I knew that if she didn't use it, she would forward it to somebody who would.

When we got back to the house, we sat at the dining room table for a while. She started to cry. I was shocked in all the years I knew Sheryl I had never seen her cry. She always seemed so strong. I know that all the stress of her husband's illness and the car accident was starting to get to her.

I assured her that no matter what happened she would be okay. I would make sure that she and her daughter always had a place to live. We joked about being the two crazy old ladies that everyone talked about. We talked about a job that I was going to be doing on Friday. She said she wanted to help. She said she was tired of sitting around. It was making her crazy. She asked if she could bring her daughter. I told her that would be fine. Her daughter was with her all the time. Her daughter is in her late twenties. She had been born with some disabilities. Her and Sheryl were like Siamese twins; they were always together.

I gave her a big hug before I left and told her how much I loved her. I again assured her that things would work out.

It was Thursday night about 9:30 pm, I realized I hadn't heard from Sheryl. She always called the day before we were going to work to let me know she hadn't forgotten and that she would be ready.

I sent her a quick text to remind her we were going to be working in the morning.

A few minutes later I got a text back. It said, "I can't my mom passed away yesterday."

I texted her back. I said I was sorry to her that. I asked her if she needed anything. She texted back that she didn't need anything.

I went to work the next day. I told Harmony that Sheryl's mom had passed away. I knew her mother had been dealing with cancer for several years. Sheryl had gone to California several years ago to take care of her. I took care of her plants and fish while she was away.

About a week before she got home her fish died. I felt really bad.

She just laughed and said, "It's just a fish."

Her mom got better, so Sheryl came back home. I felt so bad for Sheryl. She had so much on her plate already and then to have her mother die had to be taking its toll on her. I was planning on go by that afternoon to see what I could do; before I had a chance to do that I got a call from Stacy.

She said that Sheryl had passed away. I went silent. I didn't know what to say. My heart was shattering into a million pieces.

I just got a text from her last night. This can't be real. Stacy told me that they had found Sheryl dead in her bed on Wednesday. How can this be she text me just the night before? I tried to call her husband multiple times. He wouldn't answer my calls or return my text.

I finally found out it was her daughter that had sent me the text. She had sent it from her mom's phone, so I figured it was Sheryl. My friend had been dead for two days, and I didn't even know it.

I couldn't stop crying. I cried for days. When I would go to houses that we had cleaned together, I would see her there. My heart would break all over again. I would think about some of the conversations we would have about that house. How we would make jokes about some of the things that people had in their house.

Sheryl was always giving me gifts. Once she gave me a pendant of a bumble bee, it had a card with it that told the story of the bumblebee. He is not supposed to be able to fly. His body is too large for his wings. But he doesn't know this and flies anyway. This is what she wrote on the card:

Julee, My prayer for you. Whatever
you want or need in life,
    if it is God's will may it happen for
    you! Love, Sheryl.

I have that pendent and note in my dresser
next to my bed. I have all the things she has given me
over the years displayed on my shelves.

I asked Stacy to check with the Bishop to see
when they were going to have a service. He told her
that they were going to wait until Sheryl's husband
health got better. He was still in a hospice and was
too weak to deal with the situation.

When he came home from the hospice, he
texted me and asked if I had the carpet cleaner. I
didn't answer his calls or texts for a while. He then
had his daughter start texting me. Funny how he
wanted to be replied to when he couldn't have the
courtesy to do it. I finally contacted him. I took his
carpet cleaner to the house.

They didn't have her service until after the
new year. They had her service at the church across
the street from her house. I met Stacy there. We sat in
the back.

I saw her daughter in the foyer. I went up and gave her a hug and told her how sorry I was that she lost her mama. At the end of the service, I walked up front to where Sheryl's husband was sitting. I told him I was sorry for his loss. I let him know that if he needed anything to call me. He just nodded at me.

After I had dropped off Stacy, I balled. I couldn't quit crying for what seemed like hours. I missed my best friend so much. I have lost so many people that I love. I'm not willing to let anyone get that close to me again. I don't want to go through the pain of losing anymore.

COFFEE

It was a Friday night. Sheryl had been dead three weeks and two days. I was laying on my bed thinking about her. Longing to talk to her when my phone rang. It was Blane. Why would he be calling me? I figured after the last drama fest at his house he would leave me alone.

He immediately asked me what was wrong. He could tell her something in my voice.

I said, "Nothing."

He said, "Your lying. You have been crying I can hear it in the way your voice sounds."

I said, "Yes I have been. I've lost my best friend."

He said, "Sheryl."

I said, "Yes she died three weeks ago."

He said, "I'm sorry."

Then he asked if I would like to go to coffee and talk. I agreed to go. I needed to get out of this room. My heart hurt so bad that I just needed someone to talk to. I loved her so much, and I was missing her desperately. I still do.

He was at my door within ten minutes. On the drive to the restaurant, I asked him were his girlfriend was. He told me she was out with friends. Then he said they didn't even share the same room anymore.

I thought to myself. Sure, you don't. I know you Blane, and you would never let that happen. I asked him if when he said her name if he thought of me.

He said, "Every time."

We went to Village Inn to have coffee. The coffee was nasty. It tasted burned, so we only had one cup. Talked for a bit then headed back to my house.

He came in my room when we got to my house. He gave Tiffany a bunch of kisses told her he missed and loved her. He gave me a hug good bye and said if I ever need to talk to call me.

I said, "Okay. Thanks for the coffee," then I shut my door.

I wouldn't call him if I needed to talk. I know what can happen when you are in a vulnerable position. Besides I have plenty of wonderful people, I can call on.

HE'S COMING HOME

They released Bennett from his treatment program on his 17th birthday. He was upset that they wouldn't let him out before that, but he dealt with it. I had given him a bedroom in the basement. He always wanted that room, but it had been Harmony's.

The school was out for Christmas break. He had to wait until after the break to enroll and get started. He wasn't looking forward to that. He has never liked school. The kid is very smart. If he would just apply his self, he would be able to get through without a problem.

He did great for a while. He hated being on house arrest. I let his girlfriend come over and hang out, but that just wasn't enough. He wanted to go hang, with his buddies.

We did our counseling sessions when the therapist came. Sometimes it was so uncomfortable. We would just sit there and wait for his therapist to take the lead. He would just sit there. So, we would make small talk. It was agonizing for both of us.

I got the feeling he was using. He said he wasn't. I would come home, and he would have people at the house. I would tell him that they had to go. I was trying to give him a little space, but he was pushing the limits.

One night, while I was at school Harmony, called me and asked if I had given Bennett my IPad to sell. I told her I did no such thing.

She said, "We'll he is trying to sell it online."

I hurried home. He had asked me a few days before if he could put my Dad's decorative knives in his room for decoration. I told him I didn't think it would be a good idea because I wouldn't want anyone to hurt themselves or steal them. He told me I worried too much, that they would be fine. I gave in and let him take them to his room.

When I got home, I went straight to his room. The knives were gone. I was furious. I began calling and texting him. He didn't answer or respond to my texts. I had an idea where he might be, so I drove over there. He wasn't there, but his friend that he had at my house was. I told him what happened. He looked down at the ground. I'm assuming it was because he was ashamed of what he did.

He said, "Bennett told me those were his knives, that he could do whatever he wanted with them. I pawned them."

I said, "Do you still have the pawn slip?"

He said, "Yes."

I said, "Can you take me to the pawn shop so I can buy back my Dad's knives?"

He said, "Yes."

We proceeded to the pawn shop. He kept apologizing. He said he would never have done that if he knew they weren't Bennett's. I told him it's okay. At least I'm getting them back. He was really pissed off at Bennett. He told me he would be having a very serious talk with him.

They finally drug tested him in the middle of January. It came back dirty. I already knew that it was going to be. His probation officer made arraignments for him to go back to the treatment program for the month of February instead of violating him. She was giving him another chance.

A few days before the end of January my bank card got stolen. I automatically assumed it was Bennett. He had a track record of stealing from me, so he was the first person I blamed. He was adamant that he didn't take it.

I then told my roommate that had only been there about a month about the incident. I told him Bennett would definitely be caught.

He asked me, "How?"

I told him I was going to report it to the police. I told him the police would look at surveillance cameras to see who is using the card. He started crying.

He said, "Please don't report it. I have used the card. Bennett gave it to me."

I said, "Why would you use it? Why didn't you tell me he gave it to you?"

He said, "I just wasn't thinking. I didn't look at the name on the card."

He begged me not to report it.

He said, "I will pay for everything on the card."

I said, "Okay."

I went into his room later that day because I had bought several cans of pineapple and they were all gone. Just as I suspected this guy had eaten all of my pineapple. I started looking around.

There were bills and papers all over his floor. I picked them up. I read the names on them. Some of them belonged to my other roommate; some had other people's names on them. I found a social security card that was not his. I opened his dresser drawer, and there was a syringe in it. I had no choice. I had to call the police to report the card and all the other stuff I found in his room.

I called the police. They wanted to do a report over the phone, but I insisted that they come to my house.

I invited them in once they arrived. I explained everything to them. They told me they could not enter his room without him being there. They told me that he had a felony warrant. They also told me to call them as soon as he came home. They would come back and arrest him. They took the report about the card. They gave me instructions on what to do to help with the case. I listened very closely so that I could do what they needed me to do. I waited for him to come home.

He never came home. He got arrested for something else before I had the chance to call on him. I had my other roommate bag up all of his stuff and put it out in the car tent. A few weeks later he contacted me. I told him I had pressed charges. I also told him to come get his stuff. I texted him and sent him notifications on Facebook to come get his stuff. He said he would have several times. He never did.

I felt horrible that I didn't believe Bennett. We had been having some problems. He was not listening and following the rules. When the card situation happened, I decided I had had enough.

I came home from school. Bennett had a house full of friends. I was pissed. He was supposed to go turn himself in but obviously hadn't done it. I told all of his friends to get the hell out of my house. I wasn't nice about it. I then told Bennett to get all his shit together and get out of my house. I told him he was no longer welcome in my home. I have done everything I can for you. I'm done being disrespected.

His friends helped him gather his belongings. One of his friends was halfway up the stairs when he turned around and threw a rude comment at me. I told him he didn't know what has been going on. That he needed to mind his own business.

I said, "I have been here for Bennett. I am the only one who has stuck by his side. Until you know what you are talking about shut up."

He continued up the stairs. I walked out and stood on the porch. All the kids were standing by the car they came in. I waited on the porch until they drove off.

I didn't hear from Bennett for several weeks. He texted me.

He said, "How can you through me away that easy?"

I said, "It was not easy. I worry about you every second of the day. I love you, Bennett. I asked you over and over again to stop doing the things that you were doing. You wouldn't listen."

He said, "I know. I'm sorry. I love you, mommy."

I said, "I love you too."

I didn't hear from him for another several weeks. I kept our line of communication open so that I could know that he was okay. I also let him know I would always be there for him. I needed him to know that I hadn't given up on him. I will never stop believing that he can succeed. I believe that everyone can do and become whatever they want to be.

He got arrested on April 28th and is now back in Detention. I don't know what is going to happen, but one thing I do know is, I will be there with him once again every step of the way. He is my son, and I love him.

We went to court. They released him to me. They took him off of probation. He is now back at home. I'm hoping that we can make things work but only time will tell.

MY QUESTION HAS BEEN ANSWERED

Back when Blane had gotten his new girlfriend, I kept asking myself the question. Does he treat her better? Does he love her? I really shouldn't have cared, but it is the human part of me that wonders those things. Is he faithful to her? Is he going to be faithful to her and if so why wasn't he with me? Does he make her have sex against her will? Probably not because he got scared when Sheryl had reported that incident.

I think we all ask ourselves those things when a relationship ends and the other person begins a new one. We try to figure out what was wrong with us? Did we bring the things that happened on ourselves? What could I have done differently? I know that I didn't not do anything to deserve what happened.

On January 19th around midnight, I got a call from Blane. I was shocked. I hadn't heard from him since just before Christmas when he called me to tell me he had found some of my stuff in the back shed. He asked what I was doing?

I said, "I was sleeping. You sound upset. What's going on?"

He said, "I'm at the hospital."

I said, "Why? Are you okay? What happened?"

He said, "I'm okay. Nothing is wrong with me. My girlfriend and the other girl that is staying at my house got into a fight. My girlfriend stabbed her in the eye with a pair of scissors."

I said, "Oh my God. Why?"

He said, "My girlfriend and I were arguing. The other girl came up behind me and started saying stuff. The next thing I knew my girlfriend had grabbed the scissors of the desk and stabbed her"?

I was thinking to myself. You were probably making moves on the lady, and your girlfriend found out. I know who you are. The things you do. So, it was probably a love triangle gone bad.

I asked him if it was because something was going on between him and the other lady living there.

He said, "No. She is dating my son."

I thought to myself. Like that means anything. You got your Dad's girlfriend pregnant with your son years ago. So, what would stop you from sleeping with your son's girlfriend? Nothing. He told me he needed to go back into the hospital to check on her.

asked him what happened to his girlfriend.

e said, "She is in jail. Can I call you back?"

I said, "Yes."

He called back thirty minutes later. He said they were doing some tests and would probably be there most of the night. I told him that I hoped his friend would be okay. I told him everything would work itself out, that I needed to go so I could get some sleep.

He said, "Thank you for talking to me. I didn't know who else to call."

I said, "No problem. I hope your night gets better."

I laid my phone back on my dresser. I laid awake for a long time. I started thinking and wondering. Why would he call me? I wondered if it because he wanted my sympathy or if he had other motives. I finally drifted off to sleep.

The next morning, I got curious. I wanted to know if his girlfriend was really in jail. I opened my computer and went to the jail inmate housing site. I typed in her name, and sure as shit, she popped right up with the charges he had said she would have.

I went about my day. I wasn't going to call him. If he wanted to talk to me, he would call me. I made it a point to not contact him, but I do return his call or text if he contacts me first. I know I should just ignore them, but I don't. I don't know why that is.

That afternoon he called me. As usual, he wanted to know what I was doing.

I said, "Nothing; just got home. Jokingly I asked him if he was buying me dinner."

He said, "Yeah I'll buy dinner. I just need to shower. Why don't you get ready and come over?"

I said, "Okay. See you in a bit."

I decided that I would put on a nice outfit and do my makeup. I arrived at his house. I walked in the back door without knocking because he already had the door open. He was sitting on the couch surfing the channels on the TV.

I took Tiffany with me. She wiggled out of my arms the minute she saw him. Then his girlfriend's dog came running up. Poor thing was wearing the cone of shame. I asked Blane why the dog had it on. He said that he had just gotten fixed. I asked him what the dog's name was. He told me, Lexi.

I said, "That's a girl name."

He said, "I know, but it is a boy."

Lexi and Tiffany ran around the house. They would jump on and off the couch. Run into the kitchen through the living then back again. They were having a blast. We left the dogs in the house to play when we left to go to dinner. I didn't know where we were going. I just let him decide.

While we were at the restaurant, we talked about what was happening with his girlfriend. He didn't know how she was going to get out. He said he wasn't willing to put up all the money for her release.

I thought to myself, "If the person I was in love with, was in jail, I would do everything I could to help them." Yet here he was out with his ex-girlfriend having dinner.

Blane, told me while we were having dinner that I had put too much blush on. That it made me look old. I just looked at him at first. In totally disbelief that he had just said that.

thought to myself. "What an asshole. He hasn't changed one bit. Still trying to make me feel insecure. Still trying to make me feel unattractive. We'll you just fucked up." My anger had just come back full force. I was now pissed. I wasn't going to let him know that though.

During dinner, he kept complaining that his back was killing him. He mentioned that he needed to get in for a massage. I told him I would rub his back for him when we got back to the house. I knew exactly where it was hurting. I had rubbed it many times. He asked me if I wanted to spend the night. I told him I couldn't. I have to go home to take care of my dogs. I just didn't want to sleep there.

When we got back to the house, Tiffany and Lexi were curled up on the couch. They looked exhausted. They must have run around the house playing the whole time we were gone.

I sat down on the couch to have a cigarette. Blane went to the bedroom and came out in his bathrobe.

I said, "Nice robe."

He said, "Yeah, I got it for Christmas."

We sat there for a few minutes then we went to his room. As we walked through the living room he pointed out all the blood stains on the carpet. He had moved his desk from the office downstairs into the living room. The blood was also in the hall and in front of the bathroom door. He asked me what he could use to get it out. I gave him a few suggestions.

I glanced in the closet. He still had all of his stuff in there. On the floor was his old robe. It was spread out.

I said, "Is that Lexi's bed?"

He said, "No. That's Lightening's".

Lightning is one of the dog's we had. When I moved out, I left him with Blane. He got him from his previous boss, so he was his.

Blane started looking for the remote to the TV. I opened the drawer on his nightstand to see if it was in there. It wasn't. But there was a red box that said Trojan's on it. I started laughing.

I said, "She makes you wear condoms."

He said, "Sometimes."

lane took off his robe. Then he laid down on the bed. I climbed on him and sat on his butt. I began rubbing his back with lotion. I had been rubbing his back for about twenty minutes. The room was very hot and stuffy because the furnace had kicked on. We hadn't turned the fan on either. I had a long sleeve shirt on. I started sweating. I took my shirt off and continued to rub his back. I began to feel dizzy. I think it was because it was so hot in the room.

I climbed off of his back. I did I told him I was done. He grabbed me and pulled me to him. He began kissing me. He laid on top of me and began rubbing my thighs. He began telling me that he missed me. How he still loves me. He began to remove my bra. I didn't say anything. I just let it happen. He then undid my pants. He then crawled back up onto the bed. He began kissing me.

My mind was going a mile a minute. What do I do? I had put myself in this position. I shouldn't have taken off my shirt. But I was so hot I felt like I was going to pass out. I closed my eyes. I began to talk to God, begging him to forgive me for what I was doing. I was amazed how quickly he finished. When he was done, he went to the bathroom to get a towel for me to clean up.

He said, "That was beautiful."

I said, "Yes it was." I didn't know what else to say.

We walked to the living room. I had a smoke. I didn't say anything. He asked why I was so quiet. I told him I was just really tired. I need to go home now so I can take care of my dogs. I just wanted to run. I was so angry at myself for putting myself in that situation. But my question had just been answered. He was still a cheater, liar, and selfish human being. I just hope that he hasn't done the things he did to me to his girlfriend, although he did just do one of them. He cheated on her.

I cried all the way home. I felt so guilty for letting that happen. I had let God down. I had been trying so hard to live by his word. I felt bad for Blane's girlfriend. She has done nothing to do deserve this. She just fell in love with someone that could not truly love her.

I prayed to God to forgive me. I know that he did. He loves all of his children and knows that we are not perfect.

He called me the next morning. He had the nerve to ask me if I sign a paper to put the house up as collateral to get his girlfriend out.

I said, "Hell no. I can't believe you would even ask me that."

He said, "We'll I had to ask. I need to tell her I tried everything I could to get her out."

Wow! What a douche bag. Has sex with me then wants me to bail his girl out of jail. He must think I'm a real fool. I'm not the fool. He is.

After I got off the phone, I just sat there on the end of my bed thinking. I thought, "How rude was that." Like I would even consider doing that.

He called me later that day to tell me that a couple of her friends were going to bail her out. I told him that was great. Good luck. He told me to call him later. I told him that I didn't think that was a good idea.

I didn't hear from him for several weeks. When he did finally call me, he told me that he wanted to give me my things that were still at the house. I told him I was going to be having surgery that week and didn't have the time. We talked about me picking it up from him at the shop on Sunday. I told him that would work out perfectly. I didn't want to go alone. I knew that I could get my daughter Ali to go with me.

SURGERY

I had my surgery on March 10th. My daughter's boyfriend picked me up after it was done. He took care of me for several days. He was awesome. He was always making sure I had something to drink, that I was comfortable and always asking if I needed anything. I stayed at their house for several days. I really enjoyed being able to spend time with all of them. My granddaughters laid on the couch with me. I was a little nervous at first when Ali told me that he was going to be taking care of me. He turned out to be a great caretaker. I'm excited about him becoming my son in May.

On Sunday, I called Blane to see when we were going to meet. He told me in a couple of hours.

I said, "Make sure you bring my table. That way I will have all of my things, and we can be done. Except for the house."

He said, "We will never be done."

I didn't say anything for a few seconds. Then I told him I would see him shortly.

When I got off the phone, I looked over at Ali.

I said, "Guess what he just said."

Ali said, "What"?

I said, "He said we will never be done."

She gave me this look like what the hell. "You're kidding me," she said.

I said, "Nope."

We went to the shop. He wasn't there yet. We decided to get a drink while we waited. He texted me to tell me he was waiting for the train. The trains by the shop were horrible. You could be stuck sitting there for a long time.

When we got back to the shop, he was there. He brought Mindy with him. At first, I thought it was his girlfriend because she was over by the field and I couldn't see that we'll because of my eye surgery.

She came walking up. We said hello to each other and gave each other a hug. We had become friends. She would come over to the house to see my roommates. We talked a few times and had mended the relationship.

Blane said my stuff was inside the shop. We all went in to get it. I asked him if they had cleaned out the front shop?

He said, "No. Why?"

I said, "Your Dad had a vase in there with sunflowers on it. I have always wanted it. If it's still there can I have it?"

He said, "Yes."

Blane, Mindy and I walked down there. It was still there. It was sitting in the cabinet. Blane got it out and gave it to me.

I told him, "Thank you." I wanted to have something of his Dad's, to remind me of him. I loved his Dad. He was always kind to me. We walked back over to the cars. I told him thank you for giving me my things. Let me know when I can get my table.

He said, "I will get a hold of you. Maybe I will just bring the table to you."

I said, "Okay."

Ali and I headed back to the house. I didn't say much on the ride back. I was feeling very exhausted. It could have been the pain pills that I had been taking that was making me feel wiped out.

MY TABLE

A few weeks later he called. He told me he had my table in the truck and wanted to bring it to me. I was on my way to school. I had signed up for extra time. I couldn't meet him right now to get it. I really wanted my table. He said that he would take it back to his house and we could try another time. I didn't want to do that., who knows when that would be.

I told him he should bring it to me at my school. He then asked if they did massage. I told him, no but they do have a hot stone treatment that would help his back.

He said, "Really."

I said, "Yes. You should call to see if you could get an appointment."

He said, "Would you be the one doing it?"

I said, "You can request me. If they don't have me booked with someone else, I will do it."

He said, "Okay. I'm going to call. What is the number?"

I gave him the number. He scheduled an appointment. I wasn't sure how I felt about it. I was definitely feeling nervous. I thought to myself this could be an opportunity for me to finally work through the anger I was still holding. He was late to his appointment. I called to see what happened to him. He said he had fallen asleep on the couch but that he was on his way now.

I was sitting downstairs with my instructors when he finally arrived. I was going to take this opportunity to release all the anger, bitterness and ill feelings I had towards him. I took him to the room. Explained to him what he needed to do to get ready for the treatment. I excused myself from the room.

I went into the lady's room and went into the handicapped stall. I stood there for several minutes praying to God. I asked him to be with me. To help me use this opportunity to rid myself of the pain, hurt, fear and all the feelings I had been bottling up inside of me.

I went back to the room. I had tapped on the door before I entered to let him know that I was coming in. I just stood there for a minute once I entered. My heart began to pound. I started sweating, and I hadn't even picked up a hot stone. I walked up to where his head was. I asked him if he was comfortable. I then began the treatment.

I prayed the whole time I was doing. I prayed to God about everything he had done to me. I asked him to help me not hate him. I asked that he would forgive me for being so unforgiving for so long. I had worked on my forgiveness several times, but it seemed like I would always take it back and start loathing him again.

After I was done giving him his treatment I walked him upstairs to the store. He paid the cashier then we went out to his truck.

He had my table in the back. I was so happy about having my table back. I know it's just wood, but it was something that linked me to Joe. We stood out in the parking lot while we had a smoke. He told me, "Thank you for the treatment that it was amazing."

I went back inside. I felt awesome. I felt like I had finally forgiven him. I know longer felt the hate in the pit of my stomach when I thought about him. I felt free.

COMPUTER TO CAMERAS

I now had all of my stuff back. He still had the computer to the surveillance system I had purchased. I wrote that off. I didn't care about that because it had no meaning, unlike the other stuff that he had.

He called me on April 18th at 5:30 am. He said he had the computer with him. He told me he had time to bring it to me if I wanted it. I told him that he could bring it. I fell back to sleep. The dogs barking woke me up. He came into my room. I sat up. I reached over and grabbed a smoke. He sat down on the end of my bed. He started teasing me about still being in bed.

I said, "It's not time for me to get up. I still have a couple of hours."

He said, "Well you are up now."

I said, "I'm going back to sleep after you leave."

He said, "Oh really".

I asked him to move out of my way. I needed to put my dogs outside to go to the bathroom. Tiffany had jumped into his lap as soon as he sat down. I came back over to my bed. I sat on the side of it. He pushed me back and started kissing me. I pushed him away. I told him I did not want to have sex with him.

He said, "I just wanted to kiss you."

He started kissing me again. Then he took his hand and started rubbing me between the legs. I grabbed ahold of his arm and tried to push it away.

I said, "Stop. What are you doing?"

He said, "I'm waking up the dragon."

I said, "No you're not. You need to stop. You are engaged."

He said, "So."

Wow, what a piece of work. He is engaged to get married and still trying to get into my pants.

He climbed on top of me and started grinding on me. I told him to get off of me, but he just kept moving.

I looked over at my picture of Jesus that is sitting on my dresser. I began praying; asking God to please stop this. I kept telling him no. I kept saying stop. It would have done me no good to scream because no one would have heard me anyway. Just as I finished asking God to help me, he stood up. He unbuttoned his pants and pulled down the zipper. Then he began tucking in his bright orange shirt.

He said, "I have got to get going, or I'm going to be late."

He looked at me and said, "I'm the worst thing that has ever happened to you." Before I could say anything, he said, "You don't have to say anything. The look in your eyes and the expression on your face says it all."

He turned to go. Then he said, "Call me later."

I didn't call him, but he did call me.

He said, "Thank you."

I said, "For what? I didn't do anything."

He said, "For just being you."

I don't understand what it was supposed to mean or what motive he had for saying it but when I think about it. I finally like being me.

MY LIFE NOW

On Sunday, May 7, 2017, my phone rang at 5:30 am. It was Blane. I didn't answer it. He called several more times. I finally answered. I had decided that I was no longer going to answer his calls. Or call him back when he did call. I need to move on with my life. I need not to allow him to keep opening those wounds.

I answered the phone because he was so persistent. He was chipper.

He said, "Wake up beautiful. It's going to be a beautiful day. I'm at the shop. You should bring me some breakfast."

I said, "No, I'm not going to bring you breakfast."

He said, "I'm just down the street."

I said, "So. I'm still not doing it. I'm going to go back to sleep."

He said, "Me and my fiancé might be breaking up."

I said, "Why?"

He said, "I wouldn't make her truck payment for her. I think she is just wanting a free ride."

I thought to myself. You're sure not going to give her one. You only do things for others if it's going to benefit you somehow.

I said, "Well that sucks."

He said, "So when are you going to be here?"

I said, "I'm not coming over there. Blane, I need to let you go. I'm moving on with my life. I have worked very hard to recovery from all the pain. Please don't contact me anymore."

Later that day I couldn't find my keys. I became very angry. I thought it was because I couldn't find my keys but after taking some time to myself, I realized that he had brought up some old feelings. That was what was really driving my rage.

I don't know if he will leave me alone. I know that I will not contact him.

I had to relive all the things he did to me while writing this book. It was horrid to live through the first time and just as bad as I had envisioned them again while writing. It was worth it. I now feel like I have been freed. God has been with me every step of the way. I had to call on him many times during the writing process. He has held me, guided me, pushed me, cheered me on, and loved me when I couldn't love myself.

I am happier today than I have ever been. I have tried to escape this world many times, but now I'm ready to face it. I know that sometimes people think that their lives are horrible. That life is not worth living. I would just like to say that things can get tough. Things happen to us that are out of our control, but life changes constantly. Things can and will get better.

If you have been thinking about suicide or planning it, I would like to ask you to GIVE LIFE A CHANCE BEFORE YOU GIVE UP ON HOPE.

Epilogue

Have you ever been in a grocery store or a line somewhere and you encounter a very angry person? Their anger makes no sense, but just stop and ask yourself, "What is going on in their life." Maybe awful things are being done to them, and the anger and pain are surfacing in other areas because they don't know how to deal with that pain that they are stuffing deep down into their soul. The hurt, sadness, hopelessness and anger are coming out and being directed everywhere else than the place it is coming from. A gentle word or a smile just may make that person's day. We are all so busy judging.

I hid behind a mask my whole life. Avoiding people so that could not see the real me. I am no longer ashamed. I hold my head high because I know that I am not perfect. I'm still a work in progress, changing and growing every day. I may get knocked down and kicked around, but you better believe I will get back up and keep going.

There is only one judge. He is the one who can heal us and save us all.

Made in the USA
San Bernardino, CA
28 May 2017